Real Life Literacy

*Classroom tools that promote real-world
reading and writing*

KATHY PATERSON

Pembroke Publishers Limited

© 2006 **Pembroke Publishers**
538 Hood Road
Markham, Ontario, Canada L3R 3K9
www.pembrokepublishers.com

Distributed in the U.S. by Stenhouse Publishers
480 Congress Street
Portland, ME 04101-3400
www.stenhouse.com

Every effort has been made to contact copyright holders for permission to
reproduce borrowed material. The publishers apologize for any such omissions
and will be pleased to rectify them in subsequent reprints of the book.

We acknowledge the financial support of the Government of Canada through
the Book Publishing Industry Development Program (BPIDP) for our
publishing activities.

We acknowledge the assistance of the OMDC Book Fund, an initiative of the
Ontario Media Development Corporation.

Library and Archives Canada Cataloguing in Publication

Paterson, Kathy, 1943-
    Real life literacy : classroom tools that promote real-world reading and writing /
Kathy Paterson.

Includes index.
ISBN 13: 978-1-55138-204-3
ISBN 10: 1-55138-204-0

    1. Reading (Elementary). 2. Reading (Secondary). 3. English
language—Composition and exercises—Study and teaching (Elementary).
4. English language—Composition and exercises—Study and teaching
(Secondary). I. Title.

LB1576.P378 2006   428.0071   C2006-902666-1

Editor: Kate Revington
Cover design: John Zehethofer
Typesetting: Jay Tee Graphics

Printed and bound in Canada
9 8 7 6 5 4 3 2 1

Contents

Rationale:
The Need for Direct Instruction

Teachers know very well that in order for real learning to occur, the material presented must be genuine, purposeful, and functional. Unfortunately, with an overcrowded curriculum and classes filled with students of a wide diversity of backgrounds and needs, providing such material is not an easy task. Somehow, every student must find a reason to learn—an intrinsic motivation—but achieving this is not easy. Dedicated teachers are constantly seeking ways to encourage this intrinsic motivation and to "turn kids on" to learning. They want to help students appreciate the value of learning and to realize that what happens in the classroom can and *should* be transferred to the rest of their lives. They strive to make learning authentic.

Teachers can address this issue by ensuring that at least *some*, if not *all*, in-class literacy activities are seen as genuine, purposeful, and functional. Teachers are aware that much of what they are required to teach seems to lack relevance for students. Surely then, there is a case for focusing, intermittently at least, on real-life literacy activities: on tasks and activities that students can readily transfer to daily living, survival, independence, and effective communication.

Is it *possible* to bring the real world into the classroom and the classroom into the real world? I believe it is, and that belief is the basic tenet of this book.

Every person, every student, requires certain fundamental literacy skills *in addition to* basic reading, writing, listening, and speaking in order to live autonomously and successfully. Too often, it is merely supposed that students will somehow acquire these other skills while teachers are busy instructing them in the merits of the metaphor and the grammar of stories. Students are not always presented with practical, real-life literacy tasks during daily language arts lessons. To compound the problem, the curriculum allows little room for teachers to veer from the main path. There seems to be a dichotomy between what teachers are required to teach and what they might like to teach.

We can improve on this situation.

Consider the first time you had to complete a detailed form, such as an application for a passport or an insurance claim. Do you remember the angst you probably felt? Yet you are an educated professional! Now put yourself in the shoes of a young person trying to deal with a similar situation, a young person without the advantage of post-secondary education and experience, and you will understand the need for the direct, explicit teaching of such literacy tasks as accurately deciphering messages, reading bus schedules, and filling in forms.

How This Book Can Help

The lessons and blackline masters in this book will facilitate instruction in dealing effectively with some of the many literacy situations that students will face in life. Most lessons can be used with all grades with minimal teacher adaptations. They assume that students will have an understanding of alphabetization and categorization, and early lessons on these themes will help ensure that.

Lessons include motivating activities, or "sets." These can be used or not, according to teachers' wishes and needs, and should be considered suggestions only. It is recognized that teachers will have many ideas of their own for turning students on to the importance of real-life literacy techniques.

Vocabulary relevant to each topic has also been included. These words and concepts are for teacher use and can be shared according to student ages and needs.

Each numbered core lesson is organized into three major parts: (1) *preparing* (plus the optional motivational activity), (2) *presenting* (information and possible teaching strategies), and (3) *practising* (follow-up activities and blackline masters). Within each lesson, there are suggestions for a sequence of strategies or teacher-led activities culminating in student practice activities. Although it would be a good idea for teachers to bring to class genuine samples of whatever is being studied, generic blackline masters will provide in-class learning and practice that can precede examination of genuine documents, such as bus schedules, phone books, and cheques.

At the end of each cluster of lessons, there are questions that supplement the teacher's ongoing evaluation of students' successes with real-life literacy tasks. These questions have been designed to access higher levels of thinking; students will be called upon to *use* the skills, strategies, and knowledge they have gained from the lessons, as well as to recall authentic and pertinent facts. Although students can work through the questions on their own, I recommend that they discuss them with partners or in small groups. The ensuing dialogue about the issues—an example of social constructivism—will be sure to benefit their learning.

The tasks that drive the real-life literacy lessons in this book represent our culture; they are another form of communication. Direct instruction in achieving them and dealing with their intricacies and even idiosyncrasies will provide students with another way to make meaning of their world.

A. Getting Ready, Going Further: Addressing Real-Life Challenges

Before students can efficiently handle the real-life literacy activities in this book, they need to be able to alphabetize, categorize, and prioritize, as well as understand the limitations of non-standard language use, as in text messaging. Of course, these skills are taught as early as Kindergarten and reinforced throughout school, and all teachers well know how to help their students in these areas. Here, I am offering suggestions and lessons in a different format than those in the rest of the book. The lessons feature a variety of ideas that allow for the authentic *practising* of foundational skills. Teachers may use them, if needed.

Alphabetizing

The ability to alphabetize, beginning with phonemic awareness and understanding of the alphabetic principle in Grade 1, is a necessary skill for life. Even if students are in higher grades, the occasional return to alphabetizing is a worthwhile review and refresher for them.

Suggested Motivational Set

The Alphabet Game: Each person in a small group or with a partner takes a turn adding to a conversation by beginning a phrase with a word that begins with the next letter of the alphabet in sequence. The teacher can provide a "theme." For example, for the theme pets:

Keeping the students on the theme, as well as prompting them with the next letter, can be a challenge, but the results are well worth the energy expended.

"**A**fter school I will take my pet for a walk."
"**B**ut how do you walk a budgie?"
"**C**an I come along and watch you walk your budgie?"
"**D**o you even have to ask?"

Practising the Skill

All of the suggestions that follow could be used at any grade.

• Brainstorm places relevant to the students, where alphabetical order is necessary. These could include telephone books, address books, dictionaries, thesauri, encyclopedias, glossaries, indexes, lists of authors' names, or books of quotations.
• Create a list of all the names of staff, students in the classroom, or family members, and write it in alphabetical order.
• Alphabetize all the commonly used items in the classroom (as for an inventory).

- Brainstorm a list of items or events related to an individual interest or theme, perhaps sports or fantasy. Put the list in alphabetical order before choosing a specific point about which to write.
- Do a survey of favorite things—foods, TV shows, songs—among classmates or family, then present to the class in alphabetized poster form. (This activity also involves important literacy skills such as interviewing, recording, analysing, and representing data.)
- Play "The Alphabet Game." (See above.)

Categorizing

Placing items, ideas, or events into categories by first determining the categories necessary is an important skill. We do this all the time when we organize our time, our thoughts, our activities—even our closets. Some students will be able to do this automatically, whereas others can benefit from practice and reinforcement. The following activities are designed to provide that in authentic, purposeful ways.

Suggested Motivational Set

The Boys & Girls Game: A good "beginning" activity for categorizing is to brainstorm the differences between boys and girls. Students of all ages love this and are eager to add their ideas. Put some of the ideas on the board, keeping in mind that this is a "fun" exercise and that students should be reminded about gender stereotyping. Include the three words "Preferences," "Abilities," and "Size," randomly mixed in with the other words. Then, ask the students to determine which of the words on the board represent categories. With partners or in groups, allow them to complete the category lists. They can be as silly and embellished as desired.

Practising the Skill

- Brainstorm for all the clothing items students own; then, organize them by color, season in which to be worn, style casual or dressy, or even where they belong in a bedroom. Encourage students to choose their own categorizing method.
- Challenge the students to think of as many different ways to categorize a list of words as they can. They can categorize using two divisions (e.g., "is/is not") or more than two divisions if applicable (e.g., "male/female/inanimate"). Words can be randomly chosen or selected from core subjects.

> **List 1:**
>
> Apple, toast, ape, toad, turtle, apricot, avocado, antelope
>
> Categories: *starts with letter "a"/ "t"; animal/food; second letter "o"/not "o"; 1 syllable/2 syllables/3 syllables*

> **List 2:**
>
> Ecosystem, water, evaporation, rain, lake, oxygen, pollution, plants, animals, people, sun, trees, mist, deforestation, mutation, clear-cutting
>
> Categories: *living/not living; to do with water/not to do with water; people controlled/not people controlled*

• Before a hiking or backpacking expedition, or prior to reading a story or leading a class discussion about hiking and backpacking, brainstorm the items required, then organize them into categories. Categories could include perishable foods, tin foods, clothing items, liquids, and survival resources. Encourage students to come up with their own categories, perhaps according to how they will transport specific items (in packs, in carry-bags, in the teacher's pack). This discussion might take place in the context of preparing to study ecosystems.

• In order to relate directly to the language arts study of story parts or story grammar, have students identify the parts of a story (the categories), then list specific points from the story that fit under each category. For example, under the setting category, words and phrases related to place, time, season, and weather could be written.

• Use the telephone Yellow Pages and discuss how these are organized according to categories. Brainstorm the many possible words to use when seeking help from this book. Often, students have difficulty locating what they are looking for in the Yellow Pages, so activities like this are helpful. For example, ask students to consider what they would look up if they wanted to do the following:
  • get a bike fixed (bicycle repair, sports equipment, sports stores …)
  • buy a gift certificate for their mom to get her nails done (beauty parlor, beauty consultants, nails, grooming, aesthetics …)
  • buy a pizza for dinner (restaurants, dining, pizza, food …)

• When planning a classroom event such as a party or field trip, brainstorm for categories—how to prepare, what to bring, what to eat, what to wear, what to spend; then, have students, in groups, think of as many items for each category as possible. As a class, determine the most important.

• Categorize the use of the school gymnasium for any given week, and put the data on a chart such as the following.

Activity	Grade	Class	Day(s)	Time
Movement	2	2C	T/R	2:00–2:30
Volleyball	6	Ms. Parker	M/W/F	9:15–10:00

Prioritizing

Most students will be familiar with prioritizing, although they may not recognize the term or even be aware of what they are doing. When considering the many types of real-life literacy that require this skill, though, it is valuable to review and reinforce the concept, and relate it to "sequencing," a term that students are usually familiar with. Prioritizing can be done together with alphabetizing, or as a separate task.

Suggested Motivational Set

The Jacket: Together with students, decide how many steps there are to putting on a simple jacket. Write the steps clearly, each step on a single piece of paper. Be sure that the steps are easy to follow, for example, "Pick up with inside facing you" as opposed to "Pick up the jacket." Then, mix the pages up and randomly draw one out. Attempt to put the jacket on according to an incorrect sequence of steps. Make a point of doing it incorrectly. For instance, put your arm in the wrong sleeve or hold the jacket upside down, unless the directions specifically say otherwise. Students will soon realize there is no way it will work. Lead the discussion to the correct order of things, to prioritizing, as well as to the importance of clear directions.

Practising the Skill

• Discuss the importance of "putting things in order." Brainstorm for where or when it is important to do this, such as in recipes or in directions. Students can be reminded of such things as "top tens" (movie stars, songs, TV shows, and so on). Draw out the idea that prioritizing helps us to make meaning of our lives. Challenge students to find other areas of their lives where prioritization is evident.

• Have students categorize their activities for an upcoming weekend and then prioritize them according to what *they* think is the most important and then what their parents/guardians or teachers would think is important. Possible categories could be free time, practice for (hockey/soccer/other), homework, and chores. (This activity helps students focus on priorities and time organization.)

• First, alphabetize, and then prioritize by favorites, uses, or any category arrived at by the students, common lists of ten, such as items of clothing, songs, movies or TV shows, books, people, personal hygiene utensils, or classroom items. (Allowing students to prioritize classroom activities, according to what they feel is the most valuable to least valuable, can be a real eye-opener.)

Determining Acceptable Language

Because our highly technological world is so absorbed with sending and receiving rapid messages, the faster the better, it seems, text messaging and its associated "shorthand" has become almost commonplace. Unfortunately, this familiarity can have a negative effect on literacy, especially on spelling, if students are not taught that what is acceptable on a cellular device may be unacceptable for forms of standard English communication. The following activities are designed primarily to draw this concept to the attention of students rather than to give them practice in text messaging, at which most are experts anyway.

Suggested Motivational Set

From Whose Point of View: Provide a list of foods, activities, or types of writing, such as the examples below. Have students discuss and categorize them according to the point of view of (a) peers, (b) adults, (c) babies, and (d) grandparents. Be aware that stereotyping can and probably will occur here. In order to create the point-of-view argument, allow it, but be prepared to discuss this issue at some time. Encourage students to choose according to "for the most part," as there will always be variations.

List 1: Pizza, tea, hamburgers, juice in a bottle, food from a blender, toast, soft drink, salad, coffee, peanut butter sandwiches, cucumber sandwiches
List 2: Knitting, playing with a rattle, reading the newspaper, watching cartoons on TV, playing video games, playing baseball, watching sports on TV, watching an opera, having afternoon tea with friends
List 3: A text message, a thank-you letter, a pop-up book, alphabet blocks, a letter asking for information, a note explaining where you are

Follow with a discussion about how we act differently in the presence of different people, and how this may translate to the ways in which we communicate with them.

Practising the Skill

• Have students figure out the meanings of a few coded words. Samples appear below.

iiiiiiiii ooooo	(circles under the eyes)
gigigigi ccccccc	(GI's overseas)
YYUR, YYUB, ICURYY4Me	(Too wise you are, too wise you be, I see you are too wise for me.)

• Point out that some people may be as confused by communications written using typical text-messaging abbreviations as they were about the words.
• Brainstorm all the typical abbreviations used in text messaging. Have groups make charts showing the standard English equivalents.
• Draw names randomly. Have each student write a text message to the person whose name was selected. Students exchange notes and write back. Encourage students to use the most radical "shorthand" possible.
• Provide students with the information below and have them write it (a) to a friend using text messaging and (b) to a grandparent. Compare the communications in a group discussion.

> *Write a note letting your friend or grandparent know that you will be visiting on April 13 and staying for three days. You will arrive at 2 p.m. by bus. You will bring a surprise and can hardly wait for the visit.*

Choosing Real-Life Literacy Themes

Once you are confident that your students have enough grounding in the skills of alphabetizing, categorizing, and prioritizing, and grasp the idea that what is acceptable in text messaging may be unacceptable in other communication forms, you can choose any of the real-life literacy lessons clustered under six themes. The six themes are these:

See Lessons 1 to 5.

Writing and deciphering messages: Lessons on notes and memos, answering machine messages, thank-you notes and invitations, classified notices and advertisements, and sequenced instructions will help students learn to write and interpret these forms of communication accurately.

See Lessons 6 to 8.

Demystifying labels: Today almost every product that can be purchased has a label describing contents, uses, cautions, and time-usage guidelines. Drawing students' attention to these labels, as well as teaching them to decipher the various symbols and codes, is important in real-life literacy.

See Lessons 9 to 13.

Purchasing and paying: Students will learn to deal with order forms, package labels, addresses and special post forms, claim forms, methods of payment, and bank books; doing so will enable them to fill in order forms and provide accurate payment information, something that they are bound to face sooner or later.

See Lessons 14 to 18.

Decoding nonfiction, product instructions, schedules, timetables, and guides: The most educated adults have trouble interpreting some of these items, sometimes simply ignoring directions or neglecting to use or appreciate available information. Direct instruction in the analysis of generic examples will be authentic and purposeful for students of all ages.

See Lessons 19 to 21.

Using personal planning tools: Students need guidance in how to deal with life and its myriad expectations and responsibilities. Learning about personal planning and time management by working with personal planners, visual calendars, address books, and personal timetables may help them meet those expectations and responsibilities.

See Lessons 22 to 25.

Creating and completing special forms: Students need to take into account their own skills, abilities, accomplishments, and educational information, and learn how to present these in special forms, including employment applications and resumés.

Within these themes, or categories, there are twenty-five core literacy lessons. You may wish to use all the lessons in a section or choose the ones that you think your students will find most helpful and relevant. Each lesson is structured in terms of preparing, presenting, and practising. Authentic reading and writing practice are provided.

How to Extend Learning in Real-Life Literacy

Each of the core literacy lessons contains specific activity ideas. Perhaps, though, you will want to do a "little more" in a particular area or wish to pursue a particular topic further.

One option is to choose a review question from one of the six end-of-section banks. Note that not all the questions in any section need be used. Just choose questions according to lessons covered in class. There is at least one question provided for each core lesson. At times, you may want to adapt the questions, to fit the needs of your students. At other times, you may use them solely as discussion starters for the whole class. The questions are intended as a resource for teachers.

Beyond asking specific questions, consider the literacy activities outlined here. You may recognize at least some of them as activities you already use in the classroom. You will find that you can incorporate most of these into the core lessons. The ideas will work well with students of any age with minimal adaptations required.

Journalling

Writing in journals is a familiar activity that can readily accompany any of the real-life literacy lessons. Students should be encouraged to respond to any new or revisited learning in personal journals. Doing this will make their learning more valid and meaningful.

Journals such as this do not require "marking"; they are the personal reflections of the students and can be shared if the students choose to do so. In addition to personal expression journals, the following also make good journal activities to supplement the real-life literacy lessons. Teachers will be able to add to this list significantly once they teach the lessons.

- Social Studies Journal
  - Keep a record of locations and landmarks. (E18)
  - Write about different modes of communication. (B1, B2)
- Mathematics Journal
  - Record problem-solving techniques and mathematical strategies. (See lessons related to purchasing and paying.)
- Science Journal
  - Categorize phylum, species, elements and such. (See Categorizing, above.)

Writing Letters

Letters reflecting the specific skills taught or reviewed can accompany almost all of the real-life literacy activities. For example, students could write a friendly letter to a peer explaining something done in class or a business letter to "cover" an employment application. The use of letter writing is an authentic activity that mirrors real life and involves the most basic elements of communication.

Planning Field Trips or Special Activities

Allow the students to do most of the planning required for a special activity. They might determine cost, transportation (if required), itinerary, and any other aspects associated with the specific activity. In addition, they could be responsible for writing any necessary letters, invitations, thank-you notes, or announcements. Involvement in this large-scale learning includes valid tasks from all of the categories discussed in this book.

Creating "Authentic" Small Businesses

A project that involves students, in small groups, with the creation and implementation of "small businesses" automatically propels them into genuine pursuits and reinforces many of the lesson objectives of this book. Here are some appropriate and authentic small businesses that students can easily handle:

- lemonade (or hot dog or candy bar) stands for special days, such as track and field days
- tutoring groups who "work" for younger students
- helper groups who do odd jobs around the school or neighborhood
- reader groups who read to younger students, seniors, or any neighbors unable to read for themselves
- news groups who collect school news and create a newspaper of events
- entertainment groups who prepare entertainment for upcoming assemblies, for open houses, or even for local seniors' homes or hospitals

Creating "Fantasy" Small Businesses

Although the theme of these small businesses is based on fantasy, the actions needed to create the businesses remain authentic. Similar to creating authentic small businesses above, groups plan and organize small businesses of their choice. (In this case, they will plan only; they will not implement the businesses.) The groups will be required to do everything from naming their businesses to working out the logistics of finance, advertising, purchasing supplies, and preparing time sheets for employees. Groups should be expected to "present" their work to the rest of the class in some form. Examples of fantasy small businesses include

- boutiques (crafts, vintage clothing, designer shoes, wooden toys)
- fast-food restaurants (other than the familiar ones)
- specialty restaurants
- special schools, perhaps of martial arts, dance, music, or art
- video games stores

Role-Playing

Most of the real-life literacy lessons lend themselves readily to role-playing. For example, students could role-play job interviews, leaving or receiving telephone or text messages, having persuasive discussions on entertainment or travel. These are just a few possibilities; you will be able to identify similar role-play activities for many other lessons. The use of role-play not only aids in understanding; it also provides an authentic application of the skill being learned.

Practising Research Skills

Many of the lessons can easily be adapted to a research-type activity. For example, students could create questionnaires about favorite television shows (see E17), do surveys on modes of transportation to and from school (see E18), collate data from questionnaires or surveys, and write and present findings into a report.

Real-Life Literacy as Practical Literacy

Twenty-five lessons in real-life literacy follow. The tasks they represent reflect our students' everyday lives. By including such tasks, we make learning relevant, purposeful, and authentic for them. We give them tools for independence. And we empower them to face at least some of the often-confusing literacy tasks of life.

Kurt Vonnegut wrote, "Beware of the man who works hard to learn something, learns it, and finds himself no wiser than before." Too often, rote-memorized facts learned in school do not make our students wiser. It is my belief that by incorporating real-life literacy skills into our Language Arts curriculum, we foster that "wiser" component. Certainly, in my first interaction with a detailed tax form, I truly wished that someone had taught me the basics of deciphering forms. Real-life literacy is practical literacy, literacy that even the "best" students benefit from being exposed to. As teachers, we have an important role to play in fostering the connection between school curriculum and learning, and what happens in life on a daily basis—in other words, in promoting real-life literacy.

B. Writing and Deciphering Messages

Have you ever considered how many messages you send and receive in a single day? Not just the quickly scribbled notes left on the fridge or in your school mailbox, but the myriad verbal and nonverbal memoranda with which everyone is constantly bombarded. When it comes to getting needs met, it is easy to understand the necessity for good *oral* communication; however, sometimes we overlook other forms of equally important authentic information transfer: these include phone messages, quick reminder notes, thank-you notes, invitations, answering machine messages, classified notices, lost and found notices, advertisements, and sequenced instructions. Sometimes, too, we overlook the importance of "getting these communications right," as with this note I once received from a conscientious parent: "If you don't get this note, let me know so I can send another one."

As adults, we deal with all forms of communication daily and without much thought. Students, too, face a daily deluge of communication and must attend to it with much less experience. This is where good teaching can come in.

Even the youngest children will find themselves needing to "leave mom a message" or to use the answering machine that quickly engages when they make a phone call. Consider the following anecdote.

Jill was six, in Grade 1, and not feeling well. At recess she decided to call her mom at work and tell her about the sore throat that was getting worse and worse. Jill was surprised when her mom's voice mail picked up. Usually she was able to speak directly to her mom on this line. Flustered, Jill stammered, "Mom, I need you for my mouth. Can you come?" Jill's mom, when she listened to the message, misunderstood Jill's request. It had sounded as if Jill had said, "I need you for my mother." Since Jill's mom knew there was a mother and daughter activity in Jill's Brownie girls group the next week, she simply smiled and reminded herself to assure Jill that she would, indeed, be her "mother" at the outing. Jill suffered at school all day.

Without instruction, simple tasks such as leaving or receiving accurate messages, whether oral or written, may seem daunting, and yet they would be effortless for teachers to teach.

Older students may be faced with responsibilities such as creating posters to help with a sale or find a lost pet, or invitations to notify others of a party or gathering. The possibilities are endless—and so are the possibilities for error. Consider the following text, which appeared on a Lost poster created by an eager eight-year-old.

> Lost! Small male with a black face. His name is Andy. 435 6712.

Who was lost? A pet? A brother? Does the phone number belong to Andy or to the person looking for Andy? Amusing as this note is, the possible negative effects of incorrect message writing are obvious. Children need to be taught the specifics of these purposeful and authentic forms of communication, these real-life literacy tactics that are so much a part of our daily lives.

William Butler Yeats, the Irish poet, wrote, "Think like a wise man but communicate in the language of the people." When the language of the people is meant to persuade, as in advertising, children benefit from specific instruction in, and practice with, its use. With the precise teaching strategies offered in this section of *Real Life Literacy*, students may learn to accurately write and interpret this very pervasive type of communication.

1. Notes and Memos

VOCABULARY

Concise: brief and to the point

Memo: short note or communication

Homonym: word sounding like another word, but spelled differently and having a different meaning

Legible: readable, decipherable

Leaving quick notes for others is an integral part of busy lives. We should not assume that students can do this successfully without guidance.

Suggested Motivational Set

On the board or overhead, write a note that is either vague or lacking in some important information. The content should reflect something of relevance to your class. For example:

> *Take out your books and open to page 35.* (What books?)

For older students, you may wish to use a note with vague or ambiguous wording. For example:

> *Mom, I have gone to grandma's because I got a pane in my head at school.* (Hidden meaning: A "pain")

Preparing

1. Brainstorm the many times, places, and ways we leave notes and memos.
2. Discuss the importance of leaving accurate notes and memos.
3. Discuss relevant vocabulary if desired.

Presenting

4. Have the whole class or small groups brainstorm ideas for effective note or memo writing.
5. Create a class chart of ideas, such as the following.
   - Include all necessary information (who, what, when, where, why).
   - Be specific.
   - Watch out for confusing words, such as homonyms.
   - Write in "phrases," omitting unnecessary words such as "and."
   - Write legibly and neatly.
   - Sign the note and record the time it was written.
   - Reread it *critically* to see if it says what you want it to say.
   - Post or place the note somewhere you know it will be seen.

Practising

6. Provide students with two or three chances to write authentic notes or memos. Here are a few suggestions:
   - After drawing names, make a written request to the person whose name you have to do something specific in the room, perhaps sharpening a pencil.
   - Write a note to the teacher requesting something.
   - Write to a parent or guardian about where you will be after school.
   - Write a reminder note to yourself about carrying out some important task.

7. Follow up by either having students deliver their notes or by having them act on the requests they have received. A student could read the note received out loud to the class and then attempt to follow the directions *exactly*. If the directions are misleading or unclear, that will be readily apparent.
8. Role-play being the speaker on the phone, allowing the students to practise taking accurate messages.

2. Answering Machine Messages

Answering machine: any device that accepts and records messages
Voice mailbox: term for a virtual mailbox, or storage area for voice messages

Since almost everyone has an answering machine, teaching students how to leave a brief, accurate message is worthwhile.

Suggested Motivational Set

Provide a vague or incomplete message for students, such as that below, and discuss.

> *"Eh …um …Yeh … I want to speak to Bill … I need him to help with the project …um …could he call me at 434 6— (slur the last 3 numbers)"*

(Who called? What project? What time was the call? What was the return number?)

Preparing

1. Ask how many people have answering machines and discuss some of the problems that occur with them. These likely include running out of time when leaving a message, not understanding the recall number because it's spoken too quickly, and hearing confusing information.
2. Discuss the relevant vocabulary, if desired.

Presenting

3. As a class, brainstorm the possible "rules" for a good message. These should include the following:
    *   Know exactly what you want to say before beginning (jot notes if necessary).
    *   Begin by giving your name and the time of the call.
    *   Succinctly provide the basic detail of the message.
    *   Say if you want the receiver to call back, and if so, suggest a possible time for the call.
    *   Speak clearly and fairly loudly.
    *   If you run out of time, call back, apologize, and complete the call.

Practising

4. Provide a possible, authentic scenario, and allow students to practise with a partner.
5. Outline the message organizer shown below on the board or on an overhead, or encourage students to create their own samples.

Message Organizer

My name & time_____

Key words or points I wish to make _____

_____

Do I expect a recall? If so, number and possible time_____

_____

3. Thank-You Notes and Invitations

RSVP: officially, "répondez s'il vous plaît"; asking for a reply
Duration: length of time or interval of the activity
Hospitality: usually refers to the welcome or generosity of someone while you are visiting their home

Dear Gramma,
Thanks for the cool stuff.
Love, Bill

Your invited!
Monday at 5:00 PM
Bring your bathing soot.
Your friend,
Katey

It is considered polite to provide a written thank-you or note of appreciation for gifts received, even when they are from relatives. In our busy society, we tend to rely on the commercial cards to the point where children may not realize that there are a few basic ideas to include even in brief communications such as these. Similarly, the writing of complete, concise, and correct invitations is an important communication skill that can readily be taught to or reinforced with students of all ages.

Suggested Motivational Set

Share either of the notes at left on the board or overhead, and discuss the obvious problems, which include missing details and incorrect spelling.

Preparing

1. With an authentic activity in mind, perhaps the sharing of some project, story, or activity with another class or with parents, explain that you are going to write invitations, as well as thank-you cards (following attendance at the activity).

Presenting

2. Brainstorm the details that should be included in both invitations and thank-you notes. These include the following:

Invitations

- Names of both the invited and the inviter
- Identification of the activity in a few, clear words
- Location, date, time, duration
- Inclusion of any items that guests might choose to bring
- Direction about whether, how, and when a reply is expected

Thank-You Notes

- Current date, as well as the date of the incident, if the note is about a specific event
- Exact description of what the note is about (e.g., gift, hospitality)
- A few words explaining how or when you will use, or have used or appreciated, whatever the note is about
- Signature with appropriate closing, such as Love, Your friend, Your niece

Practising

3. Have students write an authentic invitation, and send or deliver it.
4. After the activity, have students write authentic thank-you notes.
5. Use the blackline masters for practice, if desired, so that students can see what elements should be included.
6. Have students create attractive invitations and notes with appropriate artwork and all pertinent information.

Invitation and Thank-You Note

An Invitation

You are invited to _____

Location _____

Time: From_____ until _____

Please bring _____

RSVP _____

A Personal Thank-You

Dear _____

Thank you for

_____

_____

_____

_____

From _____

4. Classified Notices and Advertisements

It is safe to assume that every student will, at some time, be required to write an advertisement for a paper or poster, as well as to decipher a similar piece of writing. Although these may seem like simple skills, they require several steps and specific strategies for successful marketing or understanding.

Suggested Motivational Set

Put on the board or overhead the following note, and explain that it was in your mailbox, but you don't understand it. Invite interpretations.

Ms. P, U are required 2 p r n# n by pg # the bx @ *8. Impt!!! If u frt, er B tble T b d.

Any interpretations are both wrong and right. A possible interpretation might be "Ms. P, You are required to protect your Internet number by putting it in the number 8 box. This is important. If you forget, there will be trouble to deal with." However, it could also read, "Miss Pea, You are required to put your phone number by the page with the numbers at station 8. Important! If you forfeit your black table, too bad." The objective is to draw attention to the possible multiple interpretations.

Preparing

1. Bring several newspapers to school and prepare an overhead of at least one classified ad. Tell students they are going to peruse the ads to find some item that would positively add to the atmosphere of the class, assuming, of course, that money was no object. Draw to their attention the fact that there are items for sale, as well as lost and found, in the classifieds.

Presenting

2. Peruse the classified section of a local newspaper and list the many "services." These may encompass coming events, tickets available for upcoming events, thank-you notices, career development ads, Want ads for employment and from employment agencies, and ads for real-estate sales, garage sales, pet sales, and automobile sales by "year" of make.

3. Examine the ads together, drawing attention to the usual abbreviations found in a classified section.

4. Together, count the words in a few ads, and discuss the necessity for brevity (cost factor, space factor).

5. Peruse the "lost" ads and discuss how the owners of pets or missing items must be feeling and exactly what students would do if they found a lost pet. Discuss the necessary components of a Want ad, a for-sale ad, or a lost and found ad. These should include
   - identification of who, what, when, where, why (In some cases, not all five may be necessary, but this is usually a good strategy.)
   - cost (if applicable)
   - locater number and/or address

Practising

6. Have students, in small groups or with partners, peruse newspapers or magazines to devise a classroom wish list of items located for sale. After they write out in long hand the details of the item(s), they will report back to the class.

7. In a class discussion, identify items in the classroom or school that are rarely used and only "taking up space." (One class suggested "the principal," so in jest, they wrote a classified to sell him.) In partners or small groups, write ads for these items.

8. Write a Lost ad for the newspaper. Create a Lost poster with the same information, but in a slightly different, eye-catching format. The focus might be a pet, a lost object, such as a book left on a bus, or anything else the student has lost or misplaced. (One studious young man once wrote a very convincing ad for "lost homework.")

9. Use the "Lost" and "For Sale" prompts on an overhead or on the board. The "Classified Ads" blackline master can be used as an overhead or as individual worksheets with accompanying questions, such as "Where would be your best bet to buy a bike?"

"Lost" and "For Sale" Prompts

Lost

Lost _____

When lost _____

Where lost _____

Who to call _____

When to call _____

Reward? _____

For Sale

(Name of item) _____

(Description) _____

_____

_____

_____

(Color, size, make, age, condition, …) _____

_____

_____

_____

(Cost) _____

(Who, how, and when to locate) _____

_____

_____

_____

Classified Ads

FOUND: bird, Allendale area, Thurs., May 3, 1300. Call Jack 434-2573.

FREE: large, loveable, 7-year-old male cat, black and white face, plus 5-year-old, neutered female, part Siamese cat. To good home.

GARAGE SALE: multi-family, furniture, toys, recreation articles, books, misc. 118 St. Mary Cres. 2–4 p.m., Sat., June 7. Cash only.

GARAGE SALE: moving, must sell, large household items, Sun., Feb 22, 980–143 Ave. Cheques OK.

COMPUTER DESK: 8 mo. mint, large corner, 3 drawers, oak, $300.00 OBO, Karen, 788-6502 (H) 451-7098, after 6 (W) 8–5.

SPORTING GOODS: moving, home gym, bikes, skis, skates … sacrifice, 433-0056 after 6 p.m. Ask for James. $ only.

Ideas for Discussion or Independent Work
• Write out the advertisements in "long form," as in paragraphs.
• Write a story or make a short skit explaining a possible reason for the last ad. For example, why is James moving and why will he accept cash only?
• List all the abbreviations found in the ads and provide the appropriate long forms for the words.
• Choose one ad and create a poster to accompany it.
• Choose any ad and write a jingle to accompany it.
• Assume you are interested in the female cat. What specific questions might you ask about her?
• Assume you are hoping to buy used in-line skates. Which ads might be useful to you? Why?

5. Sequenced Instructions

VOCABULARY

Landmarks: using specific buildings, trees, or other similar visuals to indicate specific points when creating or following a map

Key words/Phrases: specific, concise vocabulary that enables easy following

Ingredients: components or items used in a recipe

Children often learn to read recipes fairly young, but as teachers, we cannot assume all students have had this opportunity. By modelling and scaffolding these skills, and providing for practice, we are providing real-life literacy activities for our students. Due to the similarity of both following cooking or baking directions and following any other types of directions—such as those *to* somewhere or those on *how to* put something together—I have chosen to treat them together in this section. In both cases, prioritization is called for, so a quick review of those skills may be necessary.

Suggested Motivational Set

Play "Draw-Like-Me." Partners sit back to back. Partner A draws a simple abstract on a piece of paper, then tries to get partner B to duplicate the drawing by providing verbal directions. As a rule, the most successful partners are those who present the "like-me" directions in the same order in which A originally drew the abstract. Repeating the activity a second time and providing "remember the sequence and repeat" directions improves the reproductions and leads to a discussion of the importance of sequence in directions.

Preparing

1. Encourage a discussion about either home cooking or baking, or getting a toy that required assembling. Try to get students to talk about difficulties in doing the activity. If they do not, then share a personal experience. (Make it up, if necessary.)

2. Brainstorm areas in everyday life where sequence in following directions is necessary. These might include taking several buses home, following a map, learning how to use a new toy, game, or piece of equipment, learning how to play a new team sport, following the voice prompts on a phone answering machine, learning a new math concept and, of course, following a recipe. Discuss the similarities between following directions to a location and following a recipe.

3. Tell students what you will be making. Select a recipe, such as Rice Krispies squares, or an activity that is authentic for your class, perhaps the building of a piece of science lab equipment.

Presenting

4. Remind students about the importance of following directions exactly. They must be sure not to skip steps, especially when doing something for the first time. Suggest they mentally (or physically) "check off" each step as it is completed. Discuss what to do if, for example, a step is not understood or is done incorrectly. (They might repeat the step, ask for help, or start again.)

5. Discuss the importance of using *key words and phrases*, as opposed to lengthy sentences and confusing vocabulary, when writing directions.

6. Discuss the use of "landmarks" when writing directions about how to get somewhere.

7. Provide the materials necessary so that you can model or provide scaffolding for an activity where directions are followed together. Such an activity might be the making of cookies, the solving of a problem, or the putting together of blocks in a specific design.

Practising

8. The simple directions for Rice Krispies squares are included here and can be used if desired.

> **Rice Krispies Squares**
>
> *Ingredients:*
> ½ tsp. vanilla
> ¼ cup butter (or margarine)
> 32 large marshmallows
> 4 cups Rice Krispies
>
> *Method:*
> Melt butter, vanilla, and marshmallows over low heat, stirring constantly, until marshmallows are melted. Add Rice Krispies and stir until cooled. Press into 8" × 8" pan. Cool and cut into squares.

9. Ask the students to write directions for any of the following:
   - getting from our school to _____
   - making a great sandwich
   - preparing for gym class
   - playing (any sport or game)
   - building a paper airplane
   - solving a written math problem
   - getting ready for school in the morning
   - making (spaghetti, pizza, hamburger, tacos …)

One option is to provide students with a basic blackline master. Use a numbered form with one line allotted per instruction often encourages students to be more direct and concise when writing directions. Be sure to explain that all lists are different, though; some sets of directions may need fewer or more than the number of points given in the blackline master.

Putting in Order (Sequencing)

Following Directions

Steps for _____

   1. _____

   2. _____

   3. _____

   4. _____

   5. _____

   6. _____

   7. _____

   8. _____

   9. _____

  10. _____

Steps for _____

   1. _____

   2. _____

   3. _____

   4. _____

   5. _____

   6. _____

   7. _____

   8. _____

   9. _____

  10. _____

Questions for Discussion and Review

• You have been left in charge of a younger child when you get an important phone call for your father. What will you do? You need to write down the contents of the call quickly and concisely, and still keep your eye on the child. Imagine what the message could have been and write it.

• You want to leave your friend a note explaining why you couldn't meet him or her after school as planned, and suggesting another meeting. Write the note.

• You call your neighbor to tell her you will be at her house on Saturday to help rake the leaves, but when you call, you get the answering machine. Exactly what message will you leave?

• You receive a gift from your grandmother, but the gift is not something you will ever use. You still want to express your appreciation, though. Write the thank-you note.

• You lost your new ski gloves at the park and have to create a notice in case anyone finds them. You will offer a small reward. Write the notice.

• You are hoping to get a new puppy for your birthday, and found the following ad in a paper. Your mom has told you that she is unable to pay much and that the dog must be a small variety that doesn't shed.

> Puppies for sale: Mixed breed, b & w, 2 f, 4 m. All shots. Call Kevin after 6 @ 455 9687 (h) or 974 2309 (c).

What would you ask Kevin?
What information does the advertisement give? What doesn't it give?
Would one of these puppies work for you? How do you know?

• You have been asked to assist new students and you want to make it easier for them to find their way from your classroom to the washroom, the office, and the closest exit door. Write the directions.

• You want to work after school or on weekends cutting grass. Write the ad you will place in the Classified section of the local newspaper.

• You are sending a video game to a friend by mail, but lack the instructions for playing it. You want to write out the instructions for your game. Choose a game with which you are familiar and write the instructions for playing it.

• To help your mother organize a garage sale, you agree to create an interesting invitation form that can be sent to friends and neighbors. Refreshments will be served at the sale. Create the invitation to the sale.

C. Demystifying Labels

Labels, labels everywhere—and all of them so different! Today almost every product that can be purchased has a label describing contents, uses, cautions, and time usage guidelines.

At best, labels can be perplexing; at worst, they can be ignored. How often do you play "ostrich" when faced with a particularly confusing label? Do you make believe that the label is not even there rather than try to fathom exactly what its content means to you? Now, put yourself in the innocent shoes of your students and try to imagine how bewildered they must feel in similar situations.

We can help. We can teach our students how to make sense of labels, how not to be frightened by them, but how to treat them as part of daily life.

The following anecdote reveals the bewilderment that one child felt when faced with a situation involving label interpretation.

Claire was babysitting, and not for the first time. Her two young charges seemed perfectly healthy if one could judge by their boisterousness, but at bedtime both were being medicated for colds and coughs. When Claire went to administer their medicine, though, she noticed that the label read "1 T. BID." Having no idea what that meant, Claire tried to call the children's parents, then, when unsuccessful, her own parents.

She got no answer.

After agonizing deliberation, Claire chose to not give the children any medicine, in case she gave them too much or too little. This was not a grave error, but Claire was so worried about her decision that by the time the parents returned, she was in a state of despair, feeling sure she had somehow jeopardized the health, even the lives, of the children in her custody.

Claire did not have to suffer the anxiety of being confused by a label. A knowledgeable teacher could have taught her to decipher the various real-life literacy codes and symbols commonly used on these abbreviated documents. Musician Pete Seeger once stated, "Education is when you read the fine print; experience is what you get when you don't." Teachers can help their students to not only read the fine print, but to understand it and make use of it.

As well as the labels on medicine bottles, students can be readily instructed in how to correctly decipher labels found on clothing and food items. These are broad categories and I think it's safe to say that many, if not *most* adults will admit to being confused by them at times. For example, have you ever wondered, "What does the little % sign mean on a food label?—is that important to me if I'm counting carbs?"? Or, have you asked yourself, "Does this symbol on the label in my new shirt mean that I *can* or *cannot* use bleach?"

Teachers may not be able to share with students *everything* that appears on food and clothing labels, but we can, and should, draw attention to such labels. We can also encourage students to look at labels and provide authentic practice in reading them. By so doing, we will be helping students experience a greater degree of independence and develop further competence in communicating. And isn't that what teaching is all about?

6. Medicine Container Labels

It is safe to assume that all people, at some time during their lives, will use medicines; it is also safe to assume that some people will use them incorrectly and endanger their health or their lives. In almost every home, there are bottles of vitamins. Even these, if incorrectly used, can be dangerous.

Providing practice in the correct deciphering of words written on these vials, bottles, and boxes, together with reinforcing the importance of following the directions exactly, are excellent real-life literacy strategies well worth classroom time. Although most children will not be administering medicines, even vitamins, to themselves, they will benefit from learning more about the precautions in the use of, as well as the "shorthand" used on, medicine containers. The amount of information discussed and shared with students will depend on their ages.

Suggested Motivational Set

Show overheads of two or three common-shaped medicine vials with "silly" instructions, such as the following. Discuss what details are missing or incorrect.

> *Take some every day.*
> *Eat.*
> *Expiry Date: before June*
>
> *Take as needed.*
> *Do not drink.*
> *Do not exceed 4 a day.*

Note: Be sure to point out or discuss that the expiry date is missing or incomplete (June when? Year?), that the note doesn't say whether the medicine should be taken with or before food, that the name of the person for whom the prescription was written is missing, that the direction "Do not drink" is unclear (Do not drink what? when? with the meds? alcohol? milk?), that "some" is vague, and that "Take as needed" does not note the reason.

Preparing

1. Ask students how many of them have taken medicines or vitamins. Discuss the types of medicines.
2. To prompt discussion about medicine and its use, use open-ended questions, such as "If I got a new bottle of pills today, what should I see on the bottle?"

Presenting

3. Use the pictured medicine vial label as an overhead for instructional purposes, drawing attention to the following:
   - name and phone number of dispensing pharmacy (*a*)
   - name of person for whom the prescription was prepared (*b*)
   - generic name of drug, if present (*c*)
   - correct medical name of drug (*d*)
   - RX (treatment) number (*e*)
   - name of the doctor (*f*)

- strength of drug (in mg) (*g*)
- expiry date (*h*)
- date of dispensing (*i*)
- quantity remaining (if applicable) (*j*)
- DIN number (call number for Health Plans) (*k*)
- dosage (*l*)
- number of pills in the bottle when dispensed (*m*)
- precautions for taking the drug (*n*)

4. Brainstorm for precautions and rules about taking medicine. These should include the following:
- Take the exact amount of medicine or number of pills prescribed.
- Never "share" medicine.
- Take medicine that is prescribed only for you.
- Follow exactly the information provided for taking the drug.
- Take the entire amount recommended by the doctor. Avoid stopping medicine because symptoms have abated.
- Avoid storing old medicines; get rid of them by returning them to a pharmacy.
- Avoid "mixing" medicines, such as a cough syrup with an influenza medication, unless approved by your doctor.
- Read the material that comes with a new prescription and pay attention to any suggested cautions or possible side effects.

Practising

5. With partners, review orally the rules of correct use of medicine, as well as the information found on a medicinal label.

6. Have students create imaginary "fantasy pills" for themselves, and write the bottle labels. (This activity will serve as a review for the information.)

Medicine Vial

Quik Drugs (780) 453 9759

12345–32 St. Edmonton, AB (*a*)

Rx: 876509 (*e*)   Dr. L. Smith (*f*)

OWLSEN, PAUL (*b*)   12/Oct/06 (*i*)

Take 1 tablet(s) TWICE a day (*l*)   Take with food (*n*)

SIPOFENAC EC (*c*)   75MG (*g*)

Drug Exp: April 2007 (*h*)   Qty remain: 120 TAB (*j*)

Sipofenac sodium (S-9) (*d*)   180 TAB (*m*)

DIN: 08876549 (*k*)

7. Food Product Labels

VOCABULARY

Best-before date: guidelines about when it is best to use food; most food can be eaten after the date, but may suffer from a loss of nutrients, flavor, texture, or general quality. Foods with a shelf life of less than 90 days must have the date.

Use-by date: date found on meats, dairy, and highly perishable foods; for health reasons, be sure not to eat food past its use-by date.

Serving size: amount of food to which nutrition facts on a food package relate; for example, 1 cup of cereal, 4 crackers

Fresh: food that has not been preserved by some method such as freezing, canning, salting, or drying; not stale

Fibre: roughage, found in whole-grain items; a necessary part of everyone's diet

Food additive: something added to a food to give it specific qualities; for example, vitamins and minerals; less positive additives may be artificial color, flavor, or preservatives.

See "Food Fact Vocabulary," on page 37, for more words pertaining to food and product labels.

Since a lot of information appears here, you may want to spread the lesson over a couple of classes.

The percentage refers to the percent of daily value obtained by eating one serving of a food. For example, the daily calcium requirement for schoolchildren is about 1300 mg. One cup of whole or soya milk provides 300 mg or about 23 percent of the daily

With the latest consumer interest in and concern about what people are eating, as well as alarm over the obesity rates among children, it is a good idea to help students learn to demystify food product labels. This lesson is not intended to teach good nutrition practices, but to introduce students to food labels and encourage awareness about this form of real-life literacy.

Suggested Motivational Set

Ask students to complete "Food Products Surprises," a crossword puzzle. The blackline master appears on page 00. Once students have filled in the capitalized words, discuss the answers. Students will likely place the words correctly, but may be surprised at some of the clues and answers.

Alternatively, use the word list given in "Food Products Surprises" and ask students to classify the foods as healthy or not so healthy snacks.

Solution:

Across		Down	
5	granola	1	chocolate
8	icecream	2	Power
10	carrots	3	Smarties
12	chips	4	Sunchips
13	sunflower	6	hamburger
		7	almonds
		9	banana
		11	apple

Preparing

1. Brainstorm to find out what students already know about food nutrients, additives, and product labels. Together, create a chart of information.
2. Break the class into groups, assigning each group an area to research or study. Areas of study could include calories, daily values as a percentage (see margin note), fats, sodium, protein, carbohydrates, additives, and best-before dates. The focus is for groups to define the terms in a way they can understand.

Presenting

3. Have the groups present their information to the class. Alternatively, you could provide the information (see "Food Fact Vocabulary" on page 00; the degree to which you share these definitions will depend on student ages and abilities).
4. Display the "Food Labels" blackline master on the overhead and discuss. Encourage students to consider why manufacturers include certain nutrients or daily percentages and omit others. Point out the discrepancies between the labels, and invite students to guess what food products they belong to. Answers: "A"—sports energy bar; "B"—small package of plain potato chips; "C"—shredded whole wheat cereal; "D"—vanilla ice cream

Food Products Surprises

Word List
apple
almonds
chips
Sunchips
banana
chocolate
Power
hamburger
carrots
Smarties
sunflower
granola
icecream

Note: The clues provide comparisons between the items in the list.

ACROSS

5 Mostly carbohydrates

8 Has the second most fat

10 Has the fewest calories

12 Has the most fat

13 Has as many calories as 2 small apples

DOWN

1 About the same calories as 4 or 5 apples

2 Contains protein as its first ingredient

3 Has more calories than a chocolate bar

4 Multigrain, but still high in fats & calories

6 Has the most calories

7 Contains about the same number of calories as an apple

9 Has the most potassium

11 A healthy 60 calories

For more information on recognizing the presence of certain ingredients in foods check out Appendix B: The Hidden Ingredients in Product Labels, on page 125.

The class can do any or all of the Practising activities, depending on teacher preference and student interest.

*If you wish to determine daily nutrient requirements for students, check the Canada Food Guide at http://www.hc-sc.gc.ca/fn-an/food-guide-aliment/review-examen/index_e.html.

5. Brainstorm for general rules when reading food labels. These include the following:
- The first ingredient listed is present in the largest amount; the last listed is in the least amount.
- If an ingredient is mentioned in the name of the product, for example, chicken pie, that must be the main ingredient in the product.
- Serving sizes are listed on containers, and all nutrients apply to single servings.
- Fats and sugar must be listed on labels—pay close attention to these if you are trying to lose weight.
- Be sure to read everything on a label.

6. Discuss as many of the facts on "A Word on Food Claims and Labels," including notes on best-before dates, as you choose. One way to approach the list is to write each fact on an index card and have students, in pairs or trios, randomly select a card. The small groups then spend a few minutes reading the card and discussing the piece of information. The groups then share their facts along with any pertinent thoughts they had during their brief discussions.

Practising

8. Have students, in pairs or small groups, create large posters that organize foods based on the nutrients that are listed first on the food labels.

9. As a class, create a bulletin board display of labels that students collect from a variety of "junk" foods, such as potato chips, as well as from healthier snacks and common daily foods, such as bread. The class can organize the labels in any way students choose.

10. Ask students to choose one of the four labels from the "Food Labels" blackline master. Invite them to write reviews of their chosen food from the point of view of its value to health.

11. Challenge students to collect information from as many home food items as possible. You can chart this information according to any variable you choose, such as sugar content, vitamin content, fibre content, or calories per serving. Having students record the exact serving size of different common foods is also a good idea—often an eye-opener for students.

12. Prompt students to review 10 common foods at home for the best-before or use-by dates. In small groups, they can discuss whether foods could be safely consumed after the date.

Food Fact Vocabulary

Not all calories listed are equal.

Calorie: a unit of energy, often listed on food labels; it refers to how much energy can be obtained from eating a serving of that food. Calories come from fat, protein, or carbohydrate. Anyone who eats more calories than burned will gain weight.

Empty calories: calories obtained from eating such food as donuts, cakes, cookies, and chocolate; these foods provide calories without nutrients.

Check ingredient lists for nutrients.

Nutrients: the substances that provide nourishment to the body and help keep it healthy; found in food, they help maintain life. Examples include vitamins and calcium.

Ingredient list: list of nutrients and non-nutrients (e.g., artificial flavor) within a single serving; in Canada, usually measured in grams (g) or milligrams (mg) for tiny amounts

Daily intake: the amount of a nutrient required daily, based on a 2000 calorie diet*

Percentages: when on a food label, they refer to how much of a daily intake of 2000 calories each nutrient provides

Protein: needed for strength, muscles, and organs, it is a necessary nutrient and is usually measured in grams.

Carbohydrates: the body's primary source of energy, these can be found in whole grains, fruits, vegetables, and sugars.

Know one fat from the other.

Although the word "fat," with its connection to calories, seems to have become nasty, this nutrient is essential for growth and development. What is important to note is the differences between types of fats.

Saturated fat: unhealthy, solid fats, such as those found in animal products

Unsaturated fat: liquid fats, such as oils; these are healthier than saturated fats, but should be eaten in moderation. The higher the percentage of unsaturated fats (monounsaturated and polyunsaturated) versus saturated fats the better.

Trans fat: more dangerous than saturated fats, these can be hidden under the deceiving term *hydrogenated vegetable oil*.

Reduced fat: an ambiguous term used to indicate that there is less fat than in similar products; however, the product may still contain as much as 25 g/100 g.

Low fat: less than 3 g of fat per 100 g

Fat free: less than 0.5 g of fat per 100 g; however, a fat-free food may still be high in calories due to excessive amounts of sugar.

Light: in terms of fat, generally 50 percent less fat than similar products

Food Labels

SAMPLE A
Nutrition Facts

Serving size	63 g
Energy	222 cal
Protein	9.0 g
Fat	2.4 g
Carbohydrates	41 g
Sodium	100 mg
Potassium	390 mg
Calcium	300 mg
Phosphorus	350 mg
Magnesium	75 mg
Iron	3.5 mg
Vitamins (*trace amounts*)	

SAMPLE B
Nutrition Facts

		% Daily Value
Serving size	75 g	
Calories	400	
Fat	25 g	40%
Saturated	2.5 g	14%
Trans	0.3 g	
Cholesterol	0 mg	
Sodium	750 mg	31%
Carbohydrate	38 mg	13%
Fibre	3 g	11%
Sugars	2 g	
Protein	4 g	4%
Vit. C		25%
Iron		10%

SAMPLE C
Nutrition Facts
Per 3/4 c (30 g)

		% Daily Value	Plus 2% milk
Calories	120		180
Fat	1.5 g	2%	6%
Saturated	0.3 g	1%	9%
Trans	0 g		
Cholesterol	0 mg		
Sodium	170 mg	7%	10%
Carbohydrate	24 g	8%	10%
Fibre	3 g	10%	10%
Sugars	11 g		
Protein	3 g		
Vitamin A		0%	8%
Vitamin C		0%	2%
Calcium		10%	25%
Iron		30%	30%
Vitamin D		0%	25%
Niacin		6%	15%
Folate		8%	10%
Phosphorus		8%	20%
Magnesium		15%	20%
Zinc		6%	10%

SAMPLE D
Nutrition Facts
Per 1/2 c (125 ml)

Calories	170	
Fat	8 g	
Saturated & Trans	5 g	
Cholesterol	30 mg	
Fibre	0 g	
Sugar	14 g	
Protein	2 g	
Vitamin A		6% daily value
Calcium		0%

Note: Not all nutrition labels provide the % daily value; on other labels, often some percentages are omitted if they are so small as to be deemed insignificant. Similarly, there are times when *only* the percent daily value is provided.

A Word on Food Claims and Labels

When reading labels, it is often difficult to distinguish between fact and promotional promises. Learning to read food claims critically will provide you with another real-life literacy tool. It is to your advantage to be familiar with the most common "hooks" or "catchy phrases" used to make products seem perfect. This awareness will help you make healthier choices.

• When you see the word "baked," the product may not be healthier than if fried—it just sounds better.

• If a product claims to be a good source of a nutrient, a serving should contain 10–19 percent of the daily requirements of that nutrient.

• Be cautious of catchy words, such as "Energy Source" and "Nutritious and Healthy," when they appear on packaging—instead, read the label.

• If a product claims to be healthy, it should generally be good for you—low in salt and fat, and having at least 10 percent of the daily vitamin requirements.

• If you see the word "hydrogenated" in the ingredients, avoid buying or using the product.

• You might read the label on your pet's food, too. Watch out for references to preservatives, flavoring agents, and coloring—these are without nutritional value.

• If a food is listed as being 90 percent fat free, know that this is a consumer catch. The food has 10 percent fat—a high amount.

• Check the best-before and use-by dates, especially on perishable, or easy-to-spoil, foods. Remember not to eat food past its use-by date; if you eat food after a best-before date, bear in mind that there is likely a loss in nutrients and quality.

• Sometimes, a product gives a date without the words "best-before." When you see that, assume that it is a best-before date.

• If you don't see a label at all, beware!

When Words Aren't Enough
• Although most foods with best-before dates can be eaten safely after their dates, perishable foods, such as soft cheese, may be unsafe.

• Although eggs have best-before dates, they should never be eaten after those dates. The risk of salmonella poisoning is too high.

• Even when a food has not yet reached its best-before date, use your senses to determine if it is good. Look, smell, and taste a little. Sometimes, food can spoil even before its best-before date.

8. Clothing Labels

VOCABULARY

Apparel: item of clothing

Textile: the fibre that makes up the cloth (e.g., cotton thread)

Fabric: the cloth produced by the weaving of fibres, for example, polyester, linen, or cotton

Laundering: washing

Dry cleaning: type of professional cleaning necessary for some garments

Pretreat: any action taken before clothes are laundered, for example, soaking or using stain remover

Solvent: the soap or detergent that dissolves in water and removes dirt

Dosing: using the right amount of detergent to get the best results: too little means unclean clothes; too much means unrinsed clothes.

Teaching students how to decipher and use the symbols on clothing is a valid real-life literacy project. Children are the consumers of the future. Indeed, many already purchase and launder their own clothing.

Suggested Motivational Set

Have students respond to the "Clothing Mysteries" blackline master, on page 41, either as a whole class or in partners.

Answers:
1. The *wool* sweater was washed in hot water.
2. Chlorine bleach had been accidentally splashed on the jeans.
3. A red shirt was accidentally washed with the white sweatshirt.
4. New towels were in the same wash as the red T-shirt.

Preparing

1. Ask students to talk about newly purchased or favorite clothing items with a partner, making a few notes on scrap paper.
2. Invite them to tell their partners all about one item in detail.
3. Afterwards, ask the students how many of them shared laundry instructions when describing their special items. (Most will not have done this.) Lead the discussion to the idea that they can find out how to launder a garment by reading the garment label.

Presenting

4. Show the blackline master "Sample Clothing Label" on the overhead, and discuss the symbols. (The label refers to a pair of jeans.) You might provide copies of "Clothing Labels Summary," which appears at the end of this lesson. The class could break into five groups, with each group focusing on one symbol and the accompanying information. Allow the groups about ten minutes to review the information, think of clothing items that might fit each category (e.g., what might be washed at the highest temperature), and prepare to present to the class.
5. Turn to "More Clothing Labels: What Do You Think I Am?" on overhead. Invite the students to guess what items of clothing each label on the overhead might belong to. There could be a number of correct answers; the thinking process will encourage students to categorize clothing according to garment care. Discuss the importance of checking labels when purchasing new clothing. Answers to "More Clothing Labels: What Do You Think I Am?": Label 1—a 100 percent colored cotton blouse; Label 2—a hand-made wool sweater; Label 3—synthetic stretch sports pants; Label 4—a white work shirt of sturdy fabric.

Clothing Mysteries

1. Mystery of the Shrinking Sweater

Sid was given a lovely red sweater by a beloved grandmother. He wore it a few times and then put it on his tiny puppy when he took the dog for a walk. What happened to make this possible?

_____

_____

_____

_____

2. Mystery of the Holy Jeans

Kaley wore her favorite jeans every day. One day when she went to put them on, she noticed that they were covered in ugly white spots. A few of the spots even had holes in the centres. She wondered if moths were in her closet. What caused this calamity?

_____

_____

_____

_____

3. Passion Pink Mystery

Joey's white sweatshirt was great—until it turned bright pink. Joey hated that color and refused to wear the sweatshirt any more. What caused this strange occurrence?

_____

_____

_____

_____

4. Mystery of the Fuzzy Wuzzies

One day when Sal took her lovely red T-shirt from the drawer and put it on, she was dismayed to notice it was totally covered with little white fuzzies. She tried to brush them off, but they stuck like glue, ruining her shirt. What had caused this?

_____

_____

_____

_____

For information about common laundry symbols, see http://www.fairynonbio.co.uk/laundry/cl_drying.shtml#.

6. Point out that some labels simply use text to provide the necessary information. Point out, too, that labels can also identify the designer of the garment, the place where it was made, garment size, and type of fabric (e.g., 90 percent cotton/10 percent polyester), with the major component being listed first. Discuss when or why this information might be important. (People may be allergic to specific materials or need material that can retain heat or wick away perspiration for coolness. They may also be looking for stretchable or preshrunk material, or seek clothing that is wrinkle or moisture resistant.)

7. *Option:* Most teachers will likely want to follow up the discussion about clothing labels by talking about correct steps for doing laundry. Discuss how the information provided on the labels affects the procedure for doing laundry. (See "How to Do Laundry," which can be handed out or discussed.)

8. On the board write the words "whites," "darks," "lights," and "fragiles." As a class, brainstorm items that would fit into each category. (Refer to "How to Do Laundry," step 1.)

Practising

9. If possible, have students check the labels on an item of clothing, such as a jacket, and copy the symbols or washing instructions. Since they may be unable to read any label on an older garment, be prepared to offer "Clothing Labels Summary" as a general guide from which to work. Have students choose an imaginary item and then write out the steps to care for it.

10. Have students create wish lists of 10 to 20 clothing items, and then create clothing labels for some or all of them. The labels should identify fabric type, place where the clothing was made, size, and laundry instructions.

Sample Clothing Label

 (Wash at 30 degrees with medium agitation.)

 (Tumble dry on cool setting.)

 (Iron on medium setting.)

 (Do not bleach.)

Clothing Labels Summary

Note: Not all garments will use exactly the same symbols; these are the most common.

Washtub Symbol:

- The number in the symbol (e.g., 30) indicates the temperature at which the garment should be washed.

- A hand in the symbol means wash by hand.

- An X through the symbol means do not wash—dry-clean only.

- Small lines under the symbol indicate the suggested amount of agitation; no line means general agitation; a single line means medium agitation (for synthetics); a double line means gentle agitation.

Drying Symbol:

- A single square with a circle in it indicates the item may be tumble-dried; a number *in* the square indicates the suggested temperature. (Not all labels carry this number.)

- A square/circle with a single dot in the centre indicates drying at low temperature.

- A square/circle with two dots in it indicates drying at high temperature.

- A square/circle with an X through it means do not dry in a dryer.

- A square with three vertical lines in it means drip drying is recommended.

- A square with a small half moon at the top means hang to dry.

- A square with a horizontal line through it means lie flat to dry.

Ironing Symbol:

- The temperature suggested for ironing is indicated by the number of dots *in* the iron. One dot, cool; two dots, medium; three dots, hot.

- A symbol with an X through it means do not iron. (These items are usually laid flat for drying.)

- If a garment needs to be ironed inside out, the label will note this in words.

Bleach Symbol:

- If the triangle is empty or has a lowercase letter "a" in it, it can be bleached. (Remember to add the bleach to the water *before* the clothes are added.)

- If the triangle has an X through it, be sure not to bleach.

- If the triangle has 2 diagonal lines through it, use non-chlorine bleach only.

Dry Cleaning Symbol:

- The circle will usually have an uppercase letter inside it. This letter indicates the type of dry cleaning recommended. For example, *A* in a circle means "Any solvent."

More Clothing Labels: What Do You Think I Am?

Label 1

Label 2

 inside out

Label 3

Label 4

How to Do Laundry

Doing laundry in a way that cleans your clothes without harming them requires you to think about colors, remember and interpret certain symbols, and read brief bits of text on labels. That's real-life literacy!

1. Sort a pile of dirty clothing by color and delicacy of fabric.

   - Whites and very lights go together; blacks and darks go together. Greys usually go with "darks." If in doubt, wash with the darker colored load.

   - If you have several pastel or light-colored items, make a separate load.

   - Fragile items, such as lingerie, can be placed in a pillowcase, which is then tied with a knot.

   - Fuzzy items, such as new towels, should be washed separately so that lint and fuzz do not get on everything else.

   - New colored items should also be washed separately, at least for the first few times or until you are sure that their color will not run.

   - Turn sweaters inside out to prevent piling; turn jeans inside out to avoid fading.

   - Check all pockets.

2. Add soap and bleach, if required, before adding clothes to the washing machine.

3. Use hot water for whites, warm water for lights, and cold water for darks.

4. If possible, remove clothes as soon as the machine stops.

5. Put the items that can go into the dryer into the dryer and use an anti-static sheet to avoid items sticking together; hang to dry or spread out to dry any items washed in a pillowcase or classed as hand washable (some of these can be washed in special cycles in newer machines).

6. Remove items as soon as they are dry and hang at once to avoid wrinkling. Leaving clothes in the dryer overnight often means they ought to be ironed, whether anyone is willing to do it or not.

Questions for Discussion and Review

- You are visiting an elderly neighbor and he asks you to get his medicine from the bathroom and help him take his pills. What should you look for on the medicine vial?
- List five precautions for taking prescription medicine.
- Your prescription from the doctor has the following written on the container.

> Take 2 tablet(s) twice a day. Take on an empty stomach.

How many tablets will you take each day? When will you take them? How will you keep accurate track of taking the pills?

- A bag of cookies has the date "May 2006" on it. It is now August 2006. Are the cookies safe to eat? How do you know? List three food items that should not be eaten after the best-before date.
- A large bag of potato chips has "Energy 350 cal." on it. You eat the entire bag because 350 cal. is not much. You then notice that the bag contains 300 g and a single serving is 30 g. Explain what has happened.
- If the first ingredient on a food label is sugar and the last is protein, what does this suggest about the food?
- You have to launder the following clothing items. Separate them into color loads: blue jeans, red T-shirt, white T-shirt, grey socks, white socks, black jeans, navy blue shirt, pale blue hooded sweatshirt, light green sports shirt.

You buy a new shirt without looking closely at the labels. You spill Coke on the shirt and want to launder it. What do the following labels tell you about how to do this?

D. Purchasing and Paying

Teachers want to enable their students to live fully, autonomously, and successfully, but they are aware that not everything they are required to teach lends itself directly to these ends.

Instruction in purchasing and paying does! Contained in this section of *Real Life Literacy* are lessons dealing with order forms, package labels, addresses and special post forms, claim forms, methods of payment, and use of bank books. It would be impossible to go through life being ignorant in these areas, yet sometimes people possess only rudimentary knowledge, something that can cause anxiety and difficulty for them. Consider, for example, the young person who, through naivety, incorrectly places an order on the Internet, pays with a parent's account number, and ends up with something unwanted, not to mention angry parents.

In our highly technological world, where a trip to the corner store is no longer the usual way to obtain goods, direct instruction in the numerous ways to purchase and pay is warranted. I am reminded of the time I used an order form to purchase an article of clothing from a catalogue. I was young, inexperienced, and unfamiliar with accurate completion of what seemed to be an extremely daunting form. Accidentally, I put the size number in the Quantity box and, well, you can guess the results. This section will allow students to deal better with order forms, package labels, claim forms and methods of payment. Even the youngest child understands the concepts of money and buying; after receiving the instruction and practice offered here, students will certainly be more literate when it comes to such forms.

In addition, if teachers are to provide comprehensive instruction in everyday communication, the issue of using postal services correctly cannot be overlooked. Consider this anecdote about a man's dilemma on how best to send items—there are so many ways.

The elderly gentleman was in line at the postal outlet, patiently waiting his turn to mail a small box he was carrying. When he finally reached the worker behind the desk, he was asked what form of postal service he wanted.

"I just want to mail this parcel," he replied.

"General post, express post, priority courier, with or without insurance, 3–5 business days or overnight courier?" the young woman behind the counter rattled off quickly. (She had obviously been doing this for a long time.)

The gentleman looked confused, stood silently for a moment, then turned and left the scene, parcel still in tow. On his way out he muttered, "How do I know ..."

Teachers can offer their students lessons and experiences so that similar situations will not happen to them. Students can be given the tools and knowledge to correctly address letters and parcels, according to official post standards for their areas, as well as to complete special order forms with ease.

Teachers can also directly instruct students in maintaining accurate records of, for example, their own money in bank books. Personal financial record-keeping, like the other practical areas covered in this section, is an important component of independence and of real-life literacy, and one not usually addressed by the official curricula.

If, as I believe, the aim of education is not just knowledge, but action, effective living, and personal freedom, then we, as teachers, need to address ordering, labelling, paying, claiming, posting, and financial record-keeping. For educators who want to empower their students with genuine skills for effective living, these lessons cannot be undervalued.

9. Order Forms

VOCABULARY

Catalogue: a directory or list of items for purchase

Unit price: the price of a single item

Subtotal: the cost of the items before considering taxes and shipping

Shipping (postage) and handling: the costs added for packaging and sending goods

C.O.D: cash on delivery; payment of items when delivered

Invoice: a list of goods prepared or services rendered as a sales record; a bill

Catalogue number: the locator number that accompanies every item and must be included when ordering

ISBN: type of locator number unique to books; International Standard Book Number

Color/Size numbers: the appropriate numbers to indicate color choice and size, where applicable

1-800 number: a phone number that allows long distance ordering without charge for the call. (Point out that fax and phone numbers are often similar.)

Although not all order forms are identical, they have common features that can be shared with students so that their first encounters with these documents will be less confusing. Although there are similarities between hard copy and online order forms, some differences may occur.

Suggested Motivational Set

Share the following anecdote and invite discussion.

A few weeks ago, I ordered a great … [pair of shoes, TV, computer game … choose according to students' ages and interests] from a catalogue that came in the mail. I waited and waited and finally the package arrived. When I opened the box, though, all I found was a huge box of live worms. I was so mad! I thought that someone was playing a nasty trick on me so I phoned the company and demanded to speak to a representative. Well, it turned out I was the one who had made the mistake, and boy, did I feel foolish. Can you guess what I did wrong?

Answer: Wrote the incorrect catalogue number on the order

Preparing

1. Suggest the "fantasy" possibility of being able to purchase three or four large items for the classroom, without consideration of cost, and brainstorm what these might be. Examples may include a plasma TV, a comfy couch for the reading corner, a fridge filled with cold drinks, or a huge aquarium. Once students get the idea, they will have plenty of ideas.

2. Write the preferred suggestions on the board and discuss where you might be able to get them.

3. Ask who has ordered from a catalogue, the Internet, or any other source, and discuss the procedure.

4. Share a variety of catalogues. The school librarian may be able to assist by loaning book catalogues.

Presenting

5. Discuss the vocabulary and share the following information with students:
   - Even if ordering by phone, it is a good idea to complete the form first.
   - Have a form of payment ready at the time of ordering.
   - Most companies no longer provide the C.O.D. (cash on delivery) option.
   - It is a good idea to ensure that a company has a "satisfaction guaranteed" or return policy that will allow return or exchange of items.
   - If asked to describe the item, use key words only. (Practise this together.)
   - There are various methods of payment (see page 62) for paying for ordered items, with VISA and MasterCard being the most common. Discuss appropriate use of parents' credit cards. Although most stores do not accept parents' cards when children present them, some will if the children are adolescents. In some cases, personal cheques may be accepted. (See page 64.) If C.O.D. is used, discuss how this works.

6. Use the "Order Form" blackline masters as overheads or as individual handouts.

7. Discuss the online ordering criteria that usually encompass the use of "shopping baskets," "add to shopping cart," "wish list," "price," "quantity," "save for later," "delete," and "proceed to checkout."

8. Invite students to compile a list of rules for filling in an order form. Together, they should come up with ideas such as these:
- Write neatly and legibly.
- Use key words if describing an item.
- Make sure that the address is correct for shipping.
- Check the order numbers carefully. A single digit error can make a big difference.
- Calculate appropriate taxes and shipping charges into the total cost.
- Remember to include information re payment.

Practising

9. Provide students with copies of "Hard Copy Order Form." Either provide a possible list of items with accompanying fictitious catalogue numbers, or allow them to choose 5–10 fantasy items to order on their own. Possible items may include
- those related to personal development, such as clothing or hair products
- those related to a preferred sport, hobby, or craft
- those related to a favorite pet
- books, games, or DVDs
- furniture pieces to decorate a "perfect room"

Once students have created their fantasy lists, have them select their five favorite items and determine the specific details necessary to order them using the order form.

Hard Copy Order Form

Order Form

Fantasy Fun Limited
777 Mystery Road
Century City, Ontario L4T 8H9   Satisfaction Guaranteed
1-800-433 0987
Fax: 905-434 0987

Ship to (if different)

Name _____   Name _____

Address _____   Address _____

_____   _____

Phone (___)_____   Phone (___) _____

E-mail _____

Date _____

Method of payment:

VISA __   MasterCard __   American Express __   Personal Cheque __   Money Order __

Card Number _____   Expiry Date _____

Signature _____

Item	Description	ISBN/ Catalogue #	Quantity	Size/ Color	Unit Price	Total

Postage & Handling   Subtotal _____

Order total: Add postage & handling _____

$50 or less $5   Add appropriate taxes _____

$51–$100 $8   Total _____

Over $101 $15

Online Order Form

Key # (on catalogue mail label) [   ]

Billing Address (*Required) (Tab between fields)

First Name [   ] *

Last Name [   ] *

Company [   ]

Address [   ] *

Address 2 [   ]

City [   ] * Province [   ] *

Postal Code [   ] * (Example: L6H 1A6 with a space, no hyphens please)

Country [   ]

Phone [   ]

E-Mail [   ] *

Shipping Address (*Required) (Tab between fields)

[ ] **Same as Billing Address**   **Select From Address Book**

10. Package Labels, Addresses, and Special Post Forms

VOCABULARY
Return address: sender, the person who has sent the mail
Designator: descriptor of where or how an item is to be delivered
Forwarding address: an address other than the initial address written on an item; an alternate destination
Characters: the letters and numbers in an address

Too often mail fails to reach its destination, and it is not always the fault of the mail system. Human error plays a role here, making instruction in the correct way to complete labels and address forms a valid and authentic literacy task.

Suggested Motivational Set

Put the following addresses on the board or overhead, and challenge students to figure out why the mail was "lost."

Mr. J. James	*Sally Smithers*
135 St. Georges Cres.	*Apt. 22*
Toronto, Ontario	*Edmonton, AB T4T 2W3*

Preparing

1. Ask who has received mail and from whom. Discuss, paying particular attention to any parcels received or letters received from a far distance.
2. Tell students how mail often fails to reach its destination, and ask why they think this might happen. Discuss, leading discussion to the idea of accurately addressing the mail.
3. Discuss the concepts of "Return to Sender" and "No known address," as these phrases may appear on returned mail.

Presenting

4. Brainstorm, discuss, or teach the necessary parts of a package label or address, including
    * return address
    * receiver's address, plus specific "Attention to" in the case of mailing to a group or general location
    * apartment, building, or office
    * street, avenue, or road
    * city/town and postal code
    * country (especially if international mail)
5. Teach or review the common abbreviations used in addresses. See Appendix B for a complete list of these.
6. Model the correct writing of these on board or overhead, stressing the importance of both accuracy and legible writing.
7. Teach or review the correct abbreviations for specific cities, provinces, and states (e.g., AB for Alberta). Canadian and U.S. abbreviations can be found in Appendix A.
8. Directly teach or reinforce the correct completion of special post forms, such as "Shipping Label," page 57.
9. Directly teach the correct completion of addresses on envelopes, paying specific attention to the criteria provided by Canada Post for international post. Note that the main difference between international and national addresses will be the listing of the country on the last line of the international address.
    * According to Canada Post, put addresses in uppercase letters.
    * Write in ink.

- Address lines should be left justified.
- Use punctuation only in proper names.
- Return addresses should be formatted in the same fashion.
- Avoid using the # sign or "N."
- Set municipality, province, and postal code on the same line.
- Set country name on the last line.
- Do not underline characters in address block.
- If typing, use 10–12 point characters.
- Add two spaces between the province symbol and the postal code.

10. Discuss or teach the proper way to wrap and send a parcel. Points include the following:
- Seal tightly with parcel tape (not string).
- If the box is too big for the contents, pack the space with newspaper or packing material—box should not rattle.
- If you do not have a box, wrap securely with brown paper or consider purchasing a ready-to-assemble box from a postal outlet.
- Address the box on both sides.
- Be sure to include a return address.
- Write legibly using a dark pen.

Practising

11. Suggest a fictional situation such as the sending of a box of toys to needy children (perhaps in a country being studied in Social Studies or one currently in the news).

12. With the class, create an imaginary address and person in charge.

13. Provide blank labels and allow students to complete by filling in this imaginary address together with the school's return address so as to protect personal privacy.

14. Write the following information much as shown on the board. Have students transfer it to official New Address cards which can be obtained from the postal service.

> Old: Apt 23, 56 st SW Van.
>   Y7U 2E3
>
> New: 99 Basin Ave TO Ontario D4R 6T6
>
> Ruth & Darell Brown

15. Use the blackline master that follows for practice.

Shipping Label

Date _____

                                                       Year   M   D

SHIPPING COPY

Detach & apply to item

Courier

From: **Telephone** _____

Customer no.

_____

Name

_____

Address

_____

City/Prov./Postal Code

_____

Signature on delivery?

_____

To: **Telephone** _____

Customer No.

_____

Name

_____

Address

_____

City/Prov./Postal Code

_____

International and National Address Samples

International Address

B. THOMPSON
35 BRACO ST
OTTAWA ON K2L 1B6
CANADA

MS JANE JONES
RODODENDRONPLEIN 7B
3053 ES ROTTERDAM
NETHERLANDS

National Address

C. S. ELLIOTT
6 57TH E ST
N VAN BC V7L 3A3

MR. JOHN PETERS
13205 123 AVE
CALGARY AB T5N 3R7

11. Claim Forms

VOCABULARY
Merchandise: goods or products
Claim: in this case, what is being asked for

Most people have returned or exchanged items or goods, and likely experienced the frustration and annoyance of having to complete forms. Although sometimes all that is required is the signing of a name, other times an inclusive form needs to be completed. Unlike an order form, a claim form must specify the exact reason for the claim, as well as the expected remuneration, be it an exchange, money refunded or credit towards a future purchase. With more people buying items online, the probability of making claims or returning items escalates. Introducing or reinforcing the strategies for dealing with these situations is a valid, authentic literacy task.

Suggested Motivational Set

Play Fortunately/Unfortunately. Begin with a whole-class "demonstration" of the game by saying the following:

> *Fortunately, I got to school on time today.*
> *Unfortunately, I forgot my lessons for you at home.*
> *Fortunately, you all have math textbooks and we can work from them.*
> *Unfortunately, we don't usually have math today.*

In partners, let students play the game, taking turns with the "fortunately" and "unfortunately" openers, using any situations authentic to the class and its activities.

Once students have the idea, provide the following scenario: "Fortunately, I bought new skates. Unfortunately, the blade on one is loose." Encourage students to continue the sequence, then debrief by drawing out all the ideas that students came up with in order to deal with the problem. Lead the discussion to the concept of making a claim.

Preparing

1. Ask the question, "Who has ever received a gift that they had to return?" Ask a few students to share their stories. Invite students to jot down a few words about returning items or goods they have purchased or received as gifts. If they do not have personal experiences, they may refer to any they have heard about or witnessed second-hand. As a last resort, they could create an imaginary situation and write about it.
2. Students then share these ideas with partners or in small groups, and together record exactly how they went about making the returns.
3. Share some of the ideas as a group.

Presenting

4. As a class, brainstorm the steps necessary for returning goods. These may include the following: (1) return the goods or items in a condition as close to "new" as possible, with all tags still attached or at least evident, (2) take the sales slip or receipt with you if possible, (3) know exactly when the item was purchased or received, and (4) remember to be polite when presenting your case.
5. Discuss the use of key words and phrases for describing reasons for the claim.

6. Together, create a list of important points to keep in mind when making a claim, for example:
  - Write legibly.
  - Provide dates of when received and when sent.
  - Include your correct (return) address.
  - Include a photocopy (not original) of any receipts or documentation that came with merchandise.
  - Clearly describe merchandise.
  - Clearly describe the problem.
  - Specifically state what you expect to be done.
  - Address properly and affix correct postage.
  - Include a self-addressed stamped envelope if you are expecting a return letter or cheque.
  - Sign the form.

7. Using the "Claim Form" blackline master on an overhead projector, fill in the form together.

Practising

8. Provide each student with a copy of the "Claim Form" blackline master. Then, either present them with an authentic situation from your classroom, perhaps a faulty piece of equipment or a book that failed to live up to expectations, invite them to create their own "fantasy" situations, or use the scenario below.

You ordered a new game for your computer on the 7th of last month, from _____ (local store or catalogue). It was delivered 4 days later, but arrived missing the directions, which you must have to be able to play the game. Using your own name and address, fill in the claim form, making any kind of claim you want to.

Claim Form

Please print.

Name: _____   Date: _____
        last   first   initial

Address: _____   Tel. No.: _____

City/Prov.: _____   Postal Code: _____

Type of merchandise: _____

Date ordered: _____   Date received: _____

Reason for claim: merchandise

not delivered ___   incorrect ___   damaged ___   incomplete ___

_____

Specific details

Type of claim (check one):

Cash refund ___   Exchange ___   Repair ___   Credit account ___

Mailing address (if different from above) _____

_____

_____

Signature _____

12. Methods of Payment

VOCABULARY

Expiry: the date at which the item or gift certificate is no longer valid

Fraud: deception or scheme of deceit

Signature: name, usually in cursive form, as it will appear on all official documents

"Plastic": in reference to methods of payment, this refers to a charge card, such as VISA or MasterCard

Bounced: when used with reference to cheques, the word means that the bank returned a cheque because there was not enough money in a bank account to cover the amount.

Non-negotiable: when used with reference to cheques or money orders, it means the duplicates that are meant as records and cannot be cashed.

Legal tender: cash, the form of money used in a specific country

Eventually, all students will be faced with having to provide some form of payment for items purchased from a catalogue, from the Internet, or even directly from a merchant. Teaching them the specifics of mastering this task is both purposeful and authentic. I often wonder, how many adults do not get merchandise as expected due to avoidable errors in simple tasks, such as correctly recording VISA numbers, or forgetting to sign cheques?

Suggested Motivational Set

Give each student a blank cheque from an old cheque book or a copy of the outline on page 64. Invite students to fill out their cheques for a friend or relative with something other than money, such as "15 minutes of homework help," "one hour of babysitting," or "offer to carry your books home today." Discuss the real reason for cheques and then prompt students to give out the ones they have completed.

Preparing

1. Present an authentic situation, such as the school purchase of a piece of equipment, and ask the students how the school might have paid for it.
2. Discuss how their parents or guardians pay for merchandise; try to elicit both "cheques" and "credit cards."

Presenting

3. Use the cheque blackline master provided as an overhead and point out how to fill it in correctly, being sure to discuss "memo" (bottom line beside signature), as well as the "non-negotiable duplicate" of the cheque. Discuss legibility of writing as well as signature.
4. Use the credit card blackline master as an overhead to discuss the important components: number, expiry date, name of holder.
5. Discuss C.O.D. (cash on delivery) and what that method involves—being at home when item is delivered.
6. Depending on the ages of students, discuss credit card fraud and bounced cheques. *Note:* This could be an opener to a writing assignment for children above the age of 11.
7. With the students, identify the parts of cheques or credit card forms that must be completed. These include
    - the date
    - payable to
    - amount (both written and in numerical form, being sure these two are exactly the same)
    - memo
    - signature
    - for a credit card, the card number and expiry date

Emphasize that legible writing, accuracy, and a distinctive signature are all important.

8. Discuss money orders, often called bank drafts, and their appropriate uses for large and small sums of money. Point out that like a cash withdrawal, the amount of a money order is taken from an account immediately. Compare that with the

way a cheque has to be received and cleared and how if the cheque is never cashed, there is never a debit. Discuss how to treat "buying" a money order versus issuing a personal cheque in a personal bank book.

Practising

9. Present the "Fantasy World" idea wherein students are each "awarded" $100 to spend in any way they want. They can peruse catalogues, if available, look online, or simply use their imaginations to select items. Provide both blank cheques and credit card forms for completion.

Generic Cheque, Cheque Duplicate, and Credit Card

Cheque

(Name) _____	Cheque No. 197
(Address) _____	
_____	Date _____
(Phone No.) _____	

Pay to the
Order of _____ $ _____

_____ /100 dollars

NEW BANK
21 First St.
Newbrook, ON T6E 0K9

Memo _____ _____

"123"   9877...009:897...808...3

Cheque Duplicate

(Name) _____	Cheque No. 197
(Address) _____	
_____	Date _____
(Phone No.) _____	

Pay to the
Order of _____ $ _____

_____ /100 dollars

NEW BANK
21 First St.
Newbrook, ON T6E 0K9

Memo _____ _____

"123"   9877...009:897...808...3   **Non-negotiable**

Generic Credit Card

13. Bank Books

VOCABULARY
Deposit: money that is put into an account
Withdrawal: what is taken out of an account
Balance: the difference between deposits and withdrawals
Overdraft: a special account that allows money, to a set sum, to be withdrawn even if that amount is not in the account
Overdrawn: overspent, "in the red"

Keeping track of a bank book seems like a simple task, but it is one at which many people, including myself, fail miserably. In some sense, it is a mathematics strategy, but even more, it is a combined real-life literacy and math strategy. Sharing the secrets of accurate and consistent recording of money deposits and withdrawals is authentic and valuable teaching.

Suggested Motivational Set

Share the following riddle: What kind of book can make some people happy, some sad, and others angry? *Answer:* A bank book!

Now, discuss the riddle more seriously, making students aware that people's reactions are based on how healthy and expected their bank-book balances are.

Preparing

1. Ask if anyone has ever "lost" money. (Most students will have and will be eager to share experiences.)

2. Ask if anyone has lost money from a "very safe place." Lead the discussion to the idea that some people "lose" money from their bank accounts (or at least *feel* as if they have because they didn't keep track of it).

3. Ask students how they might prevent this from happening and draw from them the idea of "recording in a book."

Presenting

4. Teach or review how to use a bank book accurately. Emphasize the following:
   • Record all deposits and withdrawals as soon as you make them.
   • Accurately record as well as figure the balance.
   • Write legibly.

5. Brainstorm reasons for keeping an accurate bank book. These might include
   • personal awareness and independence
   • avoidance of "embarrassment" due to having less funds than expected
   • sense of pride
   • record of earnings and spending for future referral

Practising

6. Provide students with a sample of deposits and withdrawals, together with the "Bank Book" blackline master. Model how to do the recording or challenge students to try it alone and then check results with a partner. Challenge pairs to make up imaginary earnings and withdrawals for spending for a set time (length of time dependent on age of students), and record them. Put pairs into groups of four and allow sharing of the creative bank books.

Bank Book

Date	Comment	Deposit	Withdrawal	Balance
		Balance Forward		

Date	Comment	Deposit	Withdrawal	Balance
		Balance Forward		

Date	Comment	Deposit	Withdrawal	Balance
		Balance Forward		

Questions for Discussion and Review

• You want to order a new pair of jeans from a catalogue. What information will you put on the order form?

• What key words would you use to describe each of the following items if ordering from a catalogue or online?

  Blue sweater that has a hood and a zippered front with 2 pockets

  Backpack—red and white with zipper top, 2 Velcro-closed side pouches, and a double carrying strap

  Boxed CD set of the first season of *Friends* (or any popular TV show), complete with an information booklet and decorative packaging

• You are ordering from a catalogue. The price of the item is $11.25. What other costs will you have to add to this when you send the money? *Note:* The answer may vary depending on where you live.

• What can you do if you receive a piece of mail that does not belong to you? It was either incorrectly addressed or delivered to the wrong address.

• Correctly organize the following information into a proper address.

> Mrs. T. Laundry, Leduc, Canada, T5R 2D6, St Albert Crescent, Apt 345

• You want to send a parcel to a pen pal in China. What do you know about writing an international address? List the points to remember.

• You bought a jacket from a catalogue and after one wearing, a seam came apart, so you are returning it. What information will you need to include with the jacket when you do so?

• Your father has given you a bank book and suggested you use it since you have been saving money for a new bike. The following is a list of your earnings and amounts spent. Record these accurately as you would in your bank book.

  Earned $5.00 shovelling snow, Nov. 12

  Earned $10.00 babysitting, Nov. 14

  Spent $6.00 at arcade, Nov. 20

  Earned $32.00 delivering flyers, Dec. 1

  Earned $10.00 babysitting, Dec. 5

  Spent $12.95 on Christmas gift for mom, Dec. 5

  Spent $1.50 on junk food, Dec. 7

• You want to send a video game to your friend who lives in a neighboring city. What do you need to remember about packaging and addressing the parcel?

• You receive a money order from a relative. What is this and how will you "cash" it?

E. Decoding Nonfiction, Product Instructions, Schedules, Timetables, and Guides

We live in a highly fast-paced, information-overloaded, entertaining world. Since most students will come to have a fair bit of leisure time as adults, instructing them in the various areas of real-life literacy that will let them take full use of this time is warranted.

Frank Herbert wrote, "The beginning of knowledge is the discovery of something we do not understand." It is possible that many adults, let alone students, do not understand how to accurately and efficiently use all manner of entertainment guides, transportation schedules, timetables and product-use instructions. Teachers can give students that knowledge and allow them to better understand their world.

If you doubt that adults experience difficulty interpreting some of these everyday, subject-specific forms of communication, think of the last time you were daunted by a massive display of in-coming and out-going train schedules, or of the sequenced "easy" directions that accompanied a put-it-together-yourself product. Recall a time when it took twice as long as it should have to assemble an object because you tried to "skip" reading the directions. I have a husband who, after a quick perusal of sequenced directions to *anything*, immediately passes me the paper and says he "can't do it." Luckily, children are not so easily put off, but they do require direct instruction in these forms of communication. Consider the following anecdote.

> *"Please, mom," Sherry begged. "I really need to take a taxi to the party."*
>
> *"Absolutely not," her mother replied. "You are old enough to take the bus. Taxis are too expensive!"*
>
> *"But Moooommmm …"*
>
> *"No, Sherry. Download the bus schedule and figure out how to get to Wendy's."*
>
> *"I already have the schedule, mom, but look at it!" The ten-year-old stepped away from her computer screen to allow her mother full view. The entire screen was filled with tiny numbers, letters, and symbols.*
>
> *"Oh," her mother said. "Confusing, isn't it?"*
>
> *"Now can I have taxi money?" Sherry asked.*

Although teachers do train students in the writing and reading of graphs and charts as part of the core curriculum, these skills and strategies do not necessarily generalize to the real-life use of timetables, schedules, and even entertainment guides.

Our world has so very much to offer in the way of entertainment, much of it free or at nominal cost, but only a small percentage of people take advantage of these diversions. I wonder if part of the reason for this is the simple lack of awareness, lack of knowledge of what is available, or even the inability to make sense of often confusing entertainment guides. For instance, not so long ago, I ended up at a local theatre, expecting a specific show at a specific time, only to find I had not only the date, but the time wrong. In my quick perusal of the entertainment guide in the local newspaper, I had "read it wrong." I had failed a simple real-life literacy test.

There is another reason for making students familiar with entertainment guides and schedules. I will never forget overhearing a group of adolescents discussing how bored they were and how they had "nothing to do." They said they were broke. I provided them with the comprehensive entertainment section from a weekend issue of the local newspaper and pointed out the numerous options available to them, many of which were free. They were amazed. They set off happily, on foot, for an ethnic street performance.

It is appropriate, then, for educators to specifically *teach* students not only about, but also how to use these real-life literacy communication tools. By so doing, we are preparing our students for independence, for more complete and successful lives, and for at least some degree of mastery over the many forms of literacy with which they will be faced.

14. Nonfiction Contents, Glossaries, Appendices, and Indexes

VOCABULARY
Index: alphabetically listed directory with accompanying page numbers that enable the reader to find specific items within the book; appears at the end of a book

Content: with specific relation to a book, the information contained within the pages

Contents: the table that summarizes the total content of the book

Glossary: alphabetized word list or dictionary of terms used in the book

Appendix: supplementary text matter that reinforces or expands upon the main theme of a nonfiction book and is placed near the end

Annotation: explanatory note

All teachers deal with the topics of tables of contents, glossaries, and indexes whenever the occasion arises in the classroom setting. Some students, though, seem to require more assistance in this area than others do; specific instruction, either as the teaching of a new skill or as a reinforcement activity, remains an authentic literacy pursuit.

Suggested Motivational Set

Create a mini-scavenger hunt. Refer to a familiar textbook, and list about ten concepts or ideas that appear in the table of contents, index, or glossary. (You might put the list on an overhead to save paper.) Students, in pairs, quickly locate all the items on the scavenger list by identifying exactly where each can be found in the book. The items can be as specific or as general as your class can handle.

Preparing

1. Share a new book with the students. Try to select a recently published nonfiction title with which the students are unfamiliar. The book should contain material of specific relevance to them, as well as a contents page, an index, a glossary, and an appendix.
2. Read parts of the contents, index, glossary, and appendix to them, and through discussion attempt to motivate an interest in the book.
3. Question students to see if they know from which parts of the book you obtained the shared information.

Presenting

4. Make overheads of a contents page, index page, glossary page, and an appendix, or use the following blackline masters as overheads. Discuss with students relevant features and details of these book parts. It is best to draw some of the information below from the students through probing questions.
   - The table of contents is found at the front of a book; the glossary and index are usually at the back.
   - The contents are more *thematic*, whereas the other two book parts are more *specific*.
   - Sometimes, a word listed in the index may appear only once on the listed page.
   - Topics can be researched by looking at the contents, glossary, and index.
   - Appendices do not appear in all books. If present, they usually add supplementary detail or information to text or a point made elsewhere in the book.

The blackline master on page 72 is from a fictional Language Arts book at about the Grades 4–8 levels. When you are reviewing it, have students identify the correlation between the contents page numbers and the index page numbers. For example, they will be able to tell that "Modifier" shows up in both reading and writing.

Practising

5. Have students, in pairs or small groups, create questions based on the contents, indexes, and glossaries of one of their own textbooks. They could then share these questions by "asking" them of another group. In this way, they will be thinking inferentially while practising use of these important parts of a book. An example of a question, based on the blackline masters that follow, would be "On what page(s) would you find an example of a well-written sentence?"
6. As a class, compare the contents pages and indexes of several different types of books, including familiar textbooks, fictional storybooks, self-help books, and poetry anthologies.

Contents and Index

Contents

Index (… M)

Glossary and Appendix

Glossary

Glossary

Acronym: shortened form in which initial letters or parts of compound words are used and often pronounced as a new word

Adjective: a word that describes or gives detail to a noun; a modifier

Adverb: a word that describes or modifies a verb, an adjective, or another adverb

Apostrophe ('): generally used to show contractions or possession

Hyphen (-): a short horizontal line that separates words or word parts

Modify: to alter, adjust, change, or expand the sense of a word or phrase

Preposition: a word that relates a noun or a pronoun to another word in the sentence; it establishes a relationship between an object and some other part of the sentence—the preposition and its object make up a prepositional phrase which can be used as a modifier.

Appendix

Appendix A

Sentence Types

Simple Sentence: one main idea (clause) with a single subject and a single predicate
  The dog ran out of the house.

Compound Sentence: two or more main ideas, or clauses, linked by a conjunction or a semicolon
  He saw the traffic and he quickly retreated.

Complex Sentence: one main clause with one or more subordinate (secondary) clauses
  As he watched the racing traffic, he suddenly saw his master.

Compound-Complex Sentence: two or more main clauses and one or more subordinate clauses
  By the time the boy reached the frightened dog, the creature had cowered in front of an oncoming truck.

15. Product Instructions

Deciphering the many pages of assembly and operating instructions can be a huge task. Obviously, we cannot "teach" to all the different types of merchandise that students are likely to encounter, but by working through some of these instructions with students, we can help them gain some insights and more confidence for dealing with instructions on their own. Similarly, by drawing attention to the importance of following *food* product instructions accurately, we are providing authentic literacy lessons.

Suggested Motivational Set

Play Pet Peeves. In pairs, students take turns quickly explaining their pet peeves and commenting on each other's. For example:

> Student A: *My pet peeve is homework.*
> Student B: *I agree,* **but** *my pet peeve is bologna for lunch.*
> Student A: *Not me. I like bologna,* **but** *another pet peeve is whiney people.*
> Student B: *Yep, I agree,* **but** *another pet peeve is having no money.*

After about five minutes, stop students and ask a few questions:

- What pet peeves did you have in common?
- How many others have the same pet peeves?
- Did you learn anything about your partner?
- Did you run out of pet peeves or did you still have lots more?
- What might this tell you about yourself? about your partner?

Tell students you have pet peeves, too, and tell them a couple. Now, share the idea that one of your major pet peeves is the directions that come with furniture or appliances that need to be assembled. These are often hard to make sense of or appear in tiny print on package labels yet must be followed precisely. Allow discussion and sharing.

Preparing

1. Encourage discussion about experiences with assembling items or products, such as new stereo equipment or a furniture piece. As a rule, students will have many amusing anecdotes to share; however, be prepared to share one of your own, if necessary. Lead the discussion to the hard copy instructions that accompany such items, as well as to the instructions that accompany many other products, such as microwaveable foods.

Presenting

2. If possible, have available the real instructions that accompanied some item, and either make an overhead for group examination, or provide individual student copies. The "Directions" blackline master can be used if authentic instructions are unavailable. Draw from students ideas for following such directions. These ideas should be included:
   - Read all the directions before beginning.
   - Have all necessary tools available (if assemblage is required).

- Start slowly, and complete each step before attempting the next. Avoid trying to speed up the process by skipping steps that may seem unnecessary.
- If you get stuck, return to the previous step and check your work.
- Remember that sequenced instructions on food products are for safety as well as for correct preparation of food.

Practising

3. Assign students the homework task of finding and bringing to school any examples of merchandise instructions. (If they can't bring the original instructions, they should "copy" them as well as possible.) Then, have them work in small groups to compare the instructions and discuss, paying attention to safety factors, difficult-to-understand directions, and possible disastrous outcomes if directions are not followed.

4. Students could then write a set of instructions on how to prepare a familiar food and another set for assembling a familiar item. Food preparation ideas include a special "cooked" sandwich, microwave-heated soup, spaghetti, pizza, and a hot drink, such as cocoa. Ideas of what to assemble include a paper airplane, an origami decoration, a specific construction from interlocking building blocks, and a model of a car, airplane, or ship.

5. Another follow-up literacy activity could be the writing of an amusing anecdote or story based on the unfortunate results of incorrectly following product instructions.

Directions

Making Microwave Popcorn

1. Remove plastic wrap carefully. Avoid cutting the popcorn bag.

2. Open bag out without tearing and place this side up in microwave.

3. When popping has finished, open away from face. Steam will escape and contents will be very hot.

Note: Although these seem like simple directions, if not followed correctly mishaps could happen. What possible accidents could happen? Brainstorm for ideas.

_____

_____

_____

_____

Assembling a Child's Toy Chair

1. Remove all pieces from cardboard packing.

2. Identify pieces using the enclosed diagram, and make sure all pieces are there. See diagram 1.

3. Insert the 2-inch joining shanks (E) in the holes (F) in the legs.

4. Attach all four legs (B) to chair seat (A), allowing the shanks to go through the holes on seat (G). See diagram 2.

5. Fasten with nuts & cover holes with wooden discs (H). See diagram 3.

6. Slide grooves in chair back (C) into matching grooves in seat. See diagram 4.

Note: Discuss these directions or use them as a basis for making illustrations of the finished product.

_____

_____

_____

_____

16. Phone Books and Yellow Pages

VOCABULARY
Acronym: a word formed by using the initials of the words in a phrase

Although this skill is a natural follow-up from learning to alphabetize, it is amazing how many students reach adolescence without really understanding the use of a phone book. They can usually locate a specific name, but are often daunted by numerous same names or names beginning with initials. They may have limited knowledge about the many "extras" offered by telephone books and the accompanying Yellow Pages, as well as about how to use these effectively. Consequently, "discovery" lessons, where the students find out about the telephone books from their areas, are authentic literacy activities.

Suggested Motivational Set

Play the Telephone Blitz game. In groups, students brainstorm and list the many uses of a telephone book. (Most students will not get further than the idea of phone numbers and addresses of people.) Allow five to ten minutes maximum; then, compare group lists to determine a "winner," if desired. Follow this with an in-depth examination of the front matter of telephone books, drawing attention to the myriad extras, such as Emergency Numbers, Community Guides, seating schematics for venues such as theatres and auditoria, Residential Services, First Aid Information, and Area Codes. Students are often amazed at how comprehensive these books are.

Preparing

1. Borrow as many phone books and Yellow Pages from the rest of the school as possible.
2. Create an authentic reason for students to use the phone books and the Yellow Pages. Such situations might be ordering pizza for a class party, locating the address of a person to be invited as a guest speaker, or finding the phone number and address of a local business.
3. Allow students time, in small groups or with partners, to experiment with locating the necessary information.

Presenting

4. As a class, debrief the ways students located the information.
5. Discuss with the class how to locate specific names when there are many similar names.
6. Teach students how to look at the first entries for each letter when seeking names that begin with initials or that are acronyms.
7. Teach or reinforce other helpful hints including these:
   - Hyphenated words are inserted alphabetically as two separate words.
   - Abbreviated words appearing in front of another word are listed as if spelled in full.
   - Letters used as names are considered words and are usually spaced and inserted alphabetically, starting with the first letter; however, if letters are together, then they appear as one word. Examples: A B C Drilling (See beginning of "A."); RST Tools (See "RST" as one word.)
   - Disregard apostrophes.
   - "The" usually follows the company name (e.g., City Park, The).
   - A title appears after full name (Smith, Raymond Dr.).

Source: Edmonton & Area Phone Book, 2005–2006

8. Use the blackline master "Phone Book Sample" as an overhead or individual worksheet. Doing so will allow you to reinforce numbers 6 and 7, and point out the differences between personal and business phone numbers, the way that same last names with initials and given names beginning with the same letters are presented, and the inclusion of fax lines.

9. Break the class into groups and assign each group one section at the beginning of the telephone book. Each group examines and reports back to the whole class about what is contained in that section. For example, one group may be assigned the "Emergency Numbers" page.

10. As a class, make a chart or list of all the extras offered by the telephone book. Come up with the general headings under which to look in the Yellow Pages for common products or commodities. Together, examine the generalized headings in the Yellow Pages and discuss the goods and services listed under some of them.

Practising

11. Provide the students with practice in locating specifics according to the generalized headings in the Yellow Pages. These could include baseballs, specialty foods, art supplies, skipping ropes, beauty products, hair stylists or barbers, school supplies, places to get a TV or computer fixed, or places to purchase flowers. Remember to point out that there may be several places to look for the same item or service.

12. Have students create a list of five to ten people, such as their dentists, doctors, friends, and relatives, then locate the phone numbers and addresses of each. Invite students to play the Speed Dial game. Provide each group with the same list of about ten names of people, goods, and services specific to your area. Groups challenge each other to be the first to find the correct phone numbers and addresses of the characters on the lists.

Remind students that not all listings include addresses. You might want to discuss alternate ways to find the locations, for example, obtaining addresses from the individuals themselves or asking businesses directly.

Phone Book Sample

B Fashion Designers

    23 Cam St.. 433 6784

    Fax Line 433 6788

BJ's Restaurant

    2201 Tudor Lane 490 7832

B-Line Tailors

    1223 –98 St 450 7896

"B" Scene Studios

    32 Whyte Ave 455 6754

B & C Bakery

    432 11908 82 Ave 455 0983

    Fax Line 455 0986

BCL Industries

    934 Abbotsford St 980 4312

B C M Express Ltd.

    8907 102 St 789 4556

BHD Instrumental

    4 11011 99St 453 2091

Baath M K 43 Gladstone Cres 453 2998

Baath Robert 123 143 St.................................... 455 6784

Babish G Howard 21 Regency Dr........................ 478 2345

Baby Marketplace Inc.

    5666 89 St. E 465 3221

    Fax Line 465 7885

Banks B 9876 123 Ave 455 3098

Banks Bob 43 876 Ave 430 9812

17. Entertainment Guides

Venue: a location or setting, often used in relation to a form of entertainment

Restricted: controlled or limited

Archive: library or collection often gathered with the intention of preserving information or artifacts

Artifact: an object of historical interest

Release: date on which an event opens

TBA: to be announced; with reference to entertainment guides, the note means that the show for that time slot has not yet been selected.

Classification: sorting or organization; with respect to films, the following classifications are relatively generic:

General (G): suitable for all audiences

Parental Guidance (PG): may not be suitable for all children

14A: under 14; must be accompanied by an adult

18A: under 18; must be accompanied by an adult

Restricted (R): must be over 18

Adult (A): must be 18 years of age or older; same as "Restricted"

STC: subject to classification

Authentic ways to deal with step 1 are to plan a field trip to a local entertainment venue that fits with your curriculum or to ask students to watch a specific educational show on television, after they find the date and time.

The samples are generic. Ideally, you would use genuine ones from your local area.

Today, people have more entertainment choices than ever before. Along with that, they need to know how to accurately interpret a myriad of schedules, agendas, and guides. Helping students understand how these guides are usually displayed is an authentic literacy activity. It can also open doors to such tasks as locating venues of interest, then writing about them, or researching all the movies showing at similar dates and times and creating comparison charts based on genres, ratings, or even costs.

Suggested Motivational Set

Break the class into groups and provide each group with a full copy of a local newspaper, preferably an edition that provides a good overview of all the entertainment features in the area (likely a weekend newspaper).

Make the following challenge: Groups have 15 minutes to find interesting places (museums, galleries, theatres, and movies); events (craft sales, concerts, and community endeavors); and other entertainment venues they could attend as a class, within the limitations of a specific date, time, and cost per student. Avoid telling students where to look in the newspapers; allow them to discover and discuss among themselves. Have the class compare findings at the end of the allotted time and discuss.

Preparing

1. Talk with students about favorite movies. Direct the discussion towards how to find out what, when, and where movies or television shows are playing.

Presenting

2. Share the blackline masters, "Entertainment Schedules" and "Community Entertainment," in the form of overheads or individual handouts. Discuss the significant points pertaining to movies and general entertainment and to television. For the former, note start times, locations, prices, where to obtain tickets, and possible descriptions of the activity; for the latter, note channels and their accompanying numerical values, the meaning of initials in italics, the start and end times of shows, as well as any other details presented by the guide.

Practising

3. Invite students to plan a field trip based on local entertainment guides, and, if possible, select one plan and carry it out. Alternatively, have groups develop a wish list of possible places to go, plan for a specific outing, and write persuasively to justify their choices.

4. Provide a homework activity based on a local television guide, for example: *"You are allowed one hour of television per day. You have to research the topic of weather patterns. Examine the guide to determine which channels and shows will most likely help you with this research, and plan your viewing time accordingly. Write your findings into a paragraph (essay, or report)."*

5. Challenge the students, in small groups, to come up with several good questions based on local entertainment guides. Example: Which TV channel has the most situational comedies per week? These questions can then be used to play a type of quiz show, where teams confront each other with their questions.

Entertainment Schedules

Movie Guide

Showtimes: Movie Guide

GATEWAY CINEMA
2950 Calgary Trail   433 5567

Corpse Bride (PG. May frighten young children) Fri., Mon.–Thurs. 7:15, 9:20; Sat.–Sun., 1, 3:15, 7:15, 9:20
Just Like Heaven (PG) Fri., Mon.–Thurs. 7:20, 9:35; Sat.–Sun. 1:05, 3:35, 7:20

CINEMA NORTH
14231 – 137 Ave.   454 6709

Prime (PG, coarse language) No passes. 2:00, 4:50, 7:35
Two for the Money (14A) Fri.–Thurs. 1:40, 4:30, 7:40, 9:35
Wallace & Gromit: The Curse of the Were-Rabbit (G) 12:30, 2:50, 5:10, 7:40
A History of Violence (18A, gory scenes throughout) Fri.–Thurs. 2:10, 4:30
North Country (14A, mature themes) 1:10, 3:50, 6:30, 9:00
Dreamer: Inspired by a True Story (G) 1:20, 4:00, 6:30, 9:30

Television Schedule

Prime Time: Sunday, October 30						
	6PM	6:30PM	7:00PM	7:30PM	8:00PM	8:30PM
2 CFRN	News (CC)		Law & Order (R)		Grey's Anatomy (N)	
17 MUCH	Video on Trial	MuchMusic Countdown		Rap City	Videoflow (cc)	
33 FOX	MBL Baseball (Live) Houston @ Chicago				to be announced	
40 HIST	Disasters of the Century		JAG (Part 1 of 2) (cc)		Things Move	Over There (N) (cc)
45 FAM	Buzz-Maggie	Naturally	Boy World (N)	**I Love Trouble ('94) Julia Roberts (N)		

Community Entertainment

What's On

THEATRESPORTS

Rapidfire Theatre changes its format and adds a new director. Every second half will contain a grudge match. Two improvisers square off head to head. The audience will judge on a scale of 1 to 5.

When: Fridays, 10 PM

Where: Varscona Theatre, 10329 83 Ave.

Tickets: $9.00, Students $8.00

Information: 488-0456

LIVE MUSIC

Free musical performances as part of the Arts Festival.

When: Sunday, 6:30–10:00 PM

Where: Main Lobby of the Trans Alta Arts Barn, 10330 83 Ave.

Information: 344-5634

SHERLOCK HOLMES

By David Belke. Based on the works of Arthur Conan Doyle.

Presented by Mayfield Dinner Theatre.

When: Until Sunday, Oct. 30

Where: 16615 109 St.

Tickets: $37.00–$72.00

Information: 455 2376

18. Transportation Schedules and Timetables

VOCABULARY

Itinerary: route, program, or schedule

Departure: leaving or going away; with reference to schedules, the location from which the trip begins

Arrival: the outset of arrival

Confirm: to prove or make sure of something, as in determining that a schedule or fare is correct

Duration: length of time required to complete the trip

Carrier: the name of the company or line (e.g., Air Canada, Greyhound Bus Lines)

Fare: the cost of the ticket(s)

Every area, whether urban or rural, will have its own means of public transportation and accompanying schedules. The biggest concerns lie in understanding the schedules that accompany the rapid transit familiar to big cities as well as the timetables for distance travel. Sooner or later, most students will have to decipher such schedules. Teaching them how to do this, or simply reinforcing what they already know, is a valuable and valid literacy task.

Suggested Motivational Set

Play Travel Lotto. Students divide blank sheets of paper into nine sections (draw two vertical lines intersecting two horizontal lines). Brainstorm as many forms of transportation as possible. It will be necessary to have at least 20 in order to create an interesting lotto, so a possible list is given here: car, bus, train, motorbike, tricycle, two-wheeler, skateboard, roller blades, feet, rowboat, ocean liner, sailboat, canoe, kayak, trailer, truck, airplane, helicopter, glider, parachute, dog sled, SUV, horse, and camel.

As students come up with words, list them on the board and also write each on small slips of previously cut-up paper. Students then pick any nine choices and fill in their lotto pages. Either the teacher or a student then draws paper slips randomly and reads them out. The first student(s) to check off every mode of transportation on their lotto boards wins.

Now, discuss the many forms of transportation possible, but focus on the one most commonly used by the students. Lead the discussion to transportation timetables and schedules.

Preparing

1. Brainstorm ways to get from one place to another by methods other than personal vehicle. List the many systems of transportation on the board; then, open a discussion about fares, schedules, and boarding locations.

Presenting

2. Make an overhead of the "City Transit Bus Schedule" blackline master or find and use authentic, local transportation schedules to teach or reinforce the use of the specific bus or rapid transit schedules for your area. In each case, make sure students understand how to read the schedules as well as where to find the schedules (usually on the Internet). Various modes of transportation will be dealt with separately.

City Transit Bus Schedule

This sample schedule applies to Bus #1 in the City of Edmonton Public Transportation Schedule.

West Edmonton Mall - Downtown - Capilano
Via: Misericordia Hospital - Meadowlark Shopping Center - Grant MacEwan College (Jasper Place) - Jasper Gates - Provincial Museum - Edmonton General Hospital - Riverdale - McNally High School - Capilano Mall
Bike Rack Equipped

CAPL	79	101	JP	JP	MDLK	WEM	WEM	MDLK	JP	JP	99	79	CAPL	Street
TC	106	JAS	TC	TC	TC	TC	TC	TC	TC	TC	102	106	TC	Avenue
2301	2267	1620	5101	5101	5301	5009	5009	5302	5110	5110	1707	2591	2301	Bus Stop #
DWB	DWB	DWB	ASB	DSB	DNB	AEB	DEB	DNB	ANB	DNB	DEB	DSB	AWB	Direction
										05:00	05:27	05:36	05:53	B
							05:13	05:20	05:28	05:30	05:57	06:06	06:23	B
				05:26	05:32	05:40	05:43	05:50	05:58	06:00	06:27	06:36	06:53	B
							05:58	06:05	06:13	06:15	06:42	06:51	07:08	B
		05:27	05:49	05:51	05:57	06:05	06:13	06:20	06:28	06:30	06:57	07:06	07:23	B
							06:28	06:35	06:43	06:45	07:12	07:21	07:38	B
05:21	05:40	05:57	06:19	06:21	06:27	06:35	06:43	06:50	06:58	07:00	07:27	07:36	07:53	B
				06:36	06:42	06:50	06:58	07:05	07:13	07:15	07:42	07:51	08:08	B
05:51	06:10	06:27	06:49	06:51	06:57	07:05	07:13	07:20	07:28	07:30	07:57	08:06	08:23	B
		06:42	07:04	07:06	07:12	07:20	07:28	07:35	07:43	07:45	08:12	08:21	08:38	B
06:21	06:40	06:57	07:19	07:21	07:27	07:35	07:43	07:50	07:58	08:00	08:27	08:36	08:53	B

Basic Steps for Using City Transit
- Find out the beginning and ending locations.
- Determine the bus number.
- Use the word cues at the top of the schedule to determine the exact route the bus will follow (e.g., JP = Jasper Place).
- Determine the bus direction (e.g., WB = westbound).
- Determine the "number" of the bus stop(s) where you will get on and off.
- Read the schedule vertically, from your bus stop down, until you find the time of day you wish to get on the bus.

3. For teaching about out-of-city bus lines, begin by showing students how to locate a schedule on the Internet. An outline of basic steps appears below.

- Begin by typing in the name of the bus line if known or by using a search engine for lines in your area.
- Bring to the screen **SCHEDULES & FARES**.
- Complete the on-screen chart (see the generic blackline master that follows).
- When the specific dates are shown, select departure time.
- Go to **FARES** to determine cost and find out where to purchase tickets; go to **LOCATIONS** to determine where the nearest bus station is. *Note:* It is always wise to purchase tickets in advance, although in some cases it is still possible to "buy on the bus." Be sure to find out this information the before departure date.

4. Discuss airline flights and train schedules, paying specific attention to how to access them on the Internet or through a travel agent. Since the schedules will be similar to the bus line schedules, albeit more detailed, a blackline master has not been provided here. A good idea would be to have students work with computers to download available information for a specific airline.

Any of the three Practising activities could be chosen.

Practising

5. The most authentic practice would be to plan a field trip within or to the nearest city and assign students the task of mapping the route by bus, LRT (light rail transit), or subway.

6. A secondary choice would be to have students, in groups, design an "imaginary fantasy holiday," using real airline or bus line schedules, write an itinerary, and report back to the class.

7. If an independent activity is desired, ask students to plan a trip to visit a friend or relative.

Internet Bus Line Information for "Out-of-City" Travel

Confirm Locations

Confirm departure location:

From: [   ]

Confirm arrival location:

To: [   ]

Departure date: [   ]

Return date: [   ]

BBL (Busy Bus Lines)

SCHEDULES:

Select Departure Schedule for | Tuesday, November 1, 2005 |

Departs	Arrives	Duration	Transfers	Carrier
08:00 am	03:15 pm	2d, 5h, 15m	2	BBL
01:30 pm	06:00 pm	2d, 2h, 30m	1	BBL

Select Return Schedule for | Thursday, December 1, 2005 |

Departs	Arrives	Duration	Transfers	Carrier
01:00 am	05:15 am	2d, 6h, 15m	1	BBL
12:30 pm	12:24 pm	2d, 2h, 15m	1	BBL
5:15 pm	6:20 pm	2d, 3h, 5m	1	BBL

d = day, h = hour, m = minutes

Questions for Discussion and Review

• Your favorite great aunt is coming for a visit and you have been asked to arrange a trip to a movie with her on the Monday afternoon of her arrival. Locate information about the movies being shown and make a decision based on time, location, and classification of movie. Also, plan transportation to and from the theatre.

• With a partner, create a schedule of a complete week in your classroom, and organize the facts in the same manner as a television guide. You will first collect data (e.g., what happens first on Monday and for how long?) and then organize it accordingly.

• You are researching bats. The book in which you are looking has the following information.

> Bats, 23, 45–53, 77, 79, 102–104, 234

On how many pages altogether can you expect to find something about bats? Which pages will probably have the most detail? How do you know?

• You are trying to find out the meaning of a word used frequently in your Science text. Suggest three places you can look. Which will probably give you the most detailed definition? Why? (*Possible answer:* glossary, dictionary, Internet; glossary will be more detailed if the word is a familiar one throughout the text.)

• Create the perfect sandwich and write the instructions on how to prepare it.

• With a partner, find ten unusual names in a phone book and write them down, but not in alphabetical order. Exchange lists with another pair. Challenge them to rewrite the names in the order they would appear in the phone book, as you rewrite their list. To make the task really tough, choose some names that begin with initials, hyphenated words, or abbreviated words.

• List the steps necessary for finding out which city transit bus will take you from the school to the local or nearest (hockey arena, museum, gallery …).

• You have had practice reading bus schedules. You and your partner are going to take a trip to (China, Russia, Australia …). You want to leave on June 25, 200_, and return in about a month. Locate choices of airlines, compare prices, routes and dates, and make a final selection. Be prepared to justify your choice to the class in the form of a brief report.

• Create an advertisement for the local Yellow Pages. Choose a service you wish to "sell," such as babysitting, gardening, delivering newspapers, or washing windows, and write key points for your small ad. Be sure to include all the necessary data and decide under which general heading your ad will be placed. For example, "babysitting" may be under "Home help."

• Create a "Fantasy Phone Book." Think of ten (or more) cartoon characters or characters from video games. Give them full names, addresses, and phone numbers. Write these exactly as they might appear in a phone book.

F. Using Personal Planning Tools

Most teachers are amazing time managers. We have to be; our jobs are multifaceted and demanding. It is true, too, that busy people get things done.

Nevertheless, there are times when, I am sure, even the most efficient educators feel they are "going in circles" and accomplishing little—these are instances of ineffective time management. For example, recall a time when you made many trips to the photocopier when one trip should have been enough or made three trips upstairs instead of one. Think back to a time when you missed an important meeting or date for no reason other than you forgot it. Bring to mind a time when you were trying to do so many things at once that nothing at all got done. These are some of the occasions where pre-planning was missing and efficient use of time not made.

Students, however, often lack even the rudimentary organizational skills necessary for effective, time-efficient living. This is especially true in today's world where we encourage children to "be involved," "be active," and "be fit," *but* get their homework done and keep up with their home responsibilities, too! Consider the following anecdote shared by a parent during a parent–teacher conference.

"My 11-year-old daughter, Bev, was notorious for never getting her homework done, always being late for everything—generally being disorganized. You should have seen her room! I tried to help her, but she always got angry and informed me that she was trying to "do everything." She belonged to a local Girls' Club, took dance lessons, enjoyed skating at the mall, loved reading, and had her favorite TV shows, but on any given day she would miss at least one planned activity and fail to even open her books.

"After a lengthy discussion, I realized she had so much to do that she was not getting anything *done. She would go to her room to do homework, then be distracted by her need to read, her desire to skate, the phone, whatever. She constantly bemoaned the fact that she wasted so much time, but didn't seem to be able to do anything about it.*

"Then you [speaking directly to the teacher] taught them how to use a daily planner. I couldn't believe the change! She started planning her time in advance, down to the minute, and keeping track of everything on her planner. She made a big planning chart that's now on the wall of her room. I had it laminated for her. She writes everything on it—even allows herself specific time to talk on the phone. I'm amazed; she doesn't veer from her plan for anything. She has become such an effective time manager she even has down time scheduled in for herself. Learning

how to use a daily planner has been one of the most valuable things Bev has ever learned at school! Thank you."

John F. Kennedy said, "We must use time as a tool, not a crutch." Let us help students to use this tool effectively and thereby have them worry less about wasted time.

Teachers know that their students need guidance in the intricacies of dealing with life and its myriad expectations and responsibilities. Nevertheless, I want to reinforce the importance of *teaching* students the skills that comprise personal planning and time management, including working with planners, visual calendars, address books, and personal timetables. Although some students will come by these skills on their own, many will not. By teaching these skills in our classrooms, we give students power!

19. Personal Planners and Visual Calendars

We live in such a hectic world that it is necessary to plan and allocate time wisely and efficiently. Busy adults would be lost without their agendas. There is value in teaching even young students to make use of this form of time organization; by the time they, too, become busy adults, using an agenda may be second nature to them. Until that time, they can use agendas and calendars to help make sense of their own, often frenzied, schedules.

Suggested Motivational Set

Share this anecdote with the class:

> *"A gentleman had been saving his entire life for a wonderful trip around the world. Every day he followed a strict routine of working and saving. Every day he watched his savings grow. Finally, he had enough money set aside to book the voyage of a lifetime. His excitement grew as the big day neared. He got to the airport very early—he didn't want to miss his plane—only to be told he had arrived late, a full day late. His plane ticket was for the previous day."*

Ask the students what the man could have done differently to ensure he had the date right. Lead the discussion to the importance of using a daily planner or visual calendar.

Preparing

1. If you have been practising the use of a daily agenda on the board, skip it for a day and when students react, discuss the value of providing the agenda. If you have not been doing this, begin today. For a few days, write a brief schedule of the day's events on the board each morning; then, discuss in the same manner as previously mentioned.
2. Brainstorm with students for all the upcoming activities for the next month. Discuss ways to help everyone remember these, as well as homework, personal responsibilities, and personal needs, such as getting a hair cut.

Presenting

3. Share a desk calendar with students and demonstrate how it helps you keep track of events. (If you don't normally use one, borrow a sample for demonstration purposes.) Point out that *in addition to* the use of a personal planner, a readily visible reminder, such as a calendar, has merit.
4. Use "Personal Daily Planner," the blackline master, as an overhead and demonstrate the best way to fill it in. Brainstorm for key points such as these:
   - Keep printing small and legible.
   - Find a system that works for you, then stick to it. (For example, highlight days with tests, or draw a red line under important activities that cannot be overlooked.)
   - Keep your planner with you at all times and transfer the information to a visual calendar as soon as possible. (In this way, you have two reminders.)
   - If there are several, prioritize tasks and responsibilities at the same time. (See pages 9–10.)
   - Avoid using shorthand or acronyms that you may later not recognize.

- Include times of appointments or activities, if pertinent.
- Check your planner on a specific day each week, perhaps Sunday evening, to review and prepare for upcoming events.

Practising

5. Provide students with handouts of blank "Personal Planner" pages and have them complete the pages accurately.

6. Provide students with additional copies and invite them to complete the week in a purely imaginative, fun-filled manner, with activities they have always wanted to do. They could follow up on this exercise by writing a story about "the perfect week."

Personal Daily Planner

Sunday (D_____/M_____) _____

_____

_____

Monday (D_____/M_____) _____

_____

_____

Tuesday (D_____/M_____) _____

_____

_____

Wednesday (D_____/M_____) _____

_____

_____

Thursday (D_____/M_____) _____

_____

_____

Friday (D_____/M_____) _____

_____

_____

Saturday (D_____/M_____) _____

_____

_____

20. Address Books

VOCABULARY:
Portable: moveable, transportable
Cull: to select or choose

Most students will be familiar with the address books affiliated with e-mail and the stored-memory phone numbers on cellphones, but unfamiliar with the "hard copy" address books they will probably use at some time, too. A lesson about effective use of these, together with practice, is an authentic literacy activity.

Suggested Motivational Set

Have students play Name-Word Tennis. In pairs, they rapidly toss names back and forth without repeating names or taking longer than a few moments to speak. They will quickly exhaust the names of classmates and will have to rely on their repertoires of other names. Debrief by pointing out that everyone knows so many people that keeping track of them all is impossible; however, we do need to keep track of those persons we may need to reach.

Preparing

1. Ask how many students have had the experience of needing to contact someone and not knowing the correct phone number or address. Since most students will suggest the e-mail or cellphone methods of contact, propose a scenario where neither of these would be available.
2. Discuss alternate ways to keep records of numbers and addresses. Have an address book available for sharing by making overheads of a few sample pages and passing the original around for individual inspection.

Presenting

3. Discuss the similarities and differences between electronic address keeping and the "old fashioned" address book.
4. In an attempt to review what students know about keeping an accurate address book, brainstorm for key points. These should include the following:
   - Order names alphabetically, last name first.
   - Print or write legibly.
   - When changing numbers or addresses, either erase the old ones or draw lines through them.
   - Be sure to keep the book up-to-date by regularly culling entries.
   - Use an address book that is small enough to be easily portable.
5. Present the "Address Book" blackline master as an overhead and fill in a few of the students' names with fictitious numbers and addresses to protect privacy.
6. Discuss other quick entries that might be included in an address book. Examples might be birthdays, anniversaries, one or two points to help you remember the specific person (e.g., teacher, Grade 4, friend of mom's).

Practising

7. Provide copies of the "Address Book" blackline master. Students complete the pages using names of friends and relatives, and fictitious numbers and addresses.
8. An alternate activity would be to provide a list of nonsense names and addresses and invite students to categorize, alphabetize, and enter these correctly.
9. As a follow-up activity, students could select any name from their mock address books and write a letter to that person about an upcoming school activity.

Address Book

Name	Address	Phone

21. Timetables for Personal Activities

VOCABULARY
Extracurricular: pertaining to activities outside of those related to school
Prioritize: to put in order of importance

Teachers are aware that students require instruction in personal timetabling for such activities as studying and homework. Many of today's children also take part in extracurricular activities, home responsibilities, and even some forms of employment. Consequently, the whole issue of timetabling becomes even more important.

Suggested Motivational Set

Play the Crazy Talk Game. In threes, students decide who will be in the "middle." The other two students will talk directly to that person, asking questions, demanding explanations and thoughts, on two entirely different topics, at the same time. For example, student A might be talking about a favorite sport, while student C is talking about a pet peeve. Student B, in the middle, must try to maintain conversations with both at once. After a few minutes, change positions so that all students get a chance in the middle. Debrief by pointing out how difficult it is to do several things at once. Lead students to the importance of timetabling and planning.

Preparing

1. Ask the question "Who knows what they will be doing tonight at 7:30?" Discuss and share what you will be doing at that time. Tell students you *know* that because you have created a personal timetable.
2. Discuss timetables, starting with the school timetables with which they are very familiar.
3. Brainstorm other timetables with which students are familiar, such as schedules for public transit, television, entertainment, or team sports practices. Discuss what could happen if these precise timetables were not adhered to.

Presenting

4. Teach or review the importance of personal timetabling. Begin by having students list all the daily after-school activities they do. The class could do this for an entire week.
5. Demonstrate how to use timetables such as the blackline master ones: "Daily Timetable" and "Weekly Timetable." Note that times are not given on the weekly timetable as these are variable.

Practising

6. Provide copies of timetable pages for students to complete. Encourage them to prioritize activities when necessary. (See pages 97–98.) They should complete the tables authentically, according to their individual activities and responsibilities, first; however, repeating the task in a humorous or fanciful manner is always fun.

Daily Timetable

DAY _____

4:00–4:30

_____

4:30–5:00

_____

5:00–5:30

_____

5:30–6:00

_____

6:00–6:30

_____

6:30–7:00

_____

7:30–8:00

_____

8:00–8:30

_____

8:30–9:00

_____

9:00–9:30

_____

9:30–10:00

_____

10:00–10:30

_____

10:30–11:00

_____

11:00–11:30

_____

11:30–12:00

_____

Weekly Timetable

	Sun.	Mon.	Tues.	Wed.	Thur.	Fri.	Sat.
Morning							
Afternoon							
Evening							

Questions for Discussion and Review

• Your mother is going to be away for the weekend. You, your dad, and your younger sibling want to clean the entire house as a surprise for her when she gets home Sunday evening. Create a timetable that will show how you will manage this and will indicate who will be responsible for each cleaning activity.

• You and three friends are running a "Dogs & Drinks" booth at a local outdoor event. You have determined that it will take one person to make the hot dogs, one person to make and pour lemonade, and one person to handle the money. Create a schedule that will indicate who will work when for the entire weekend from 8 a.m. Saturday until 4 p.m. Sunday. Remember to allow time for setting up and cleaning up, too.

• You have lost your address book. Explain how you might recollect all the important numbers, addresses, and e-mail addresses you had in it, and suggest what you will do to avoid losing your address book in the future.

• List the key points for keeping a useable address book (other than on your computer).

• List five reasons for using a daily planner.

• In your room or beside your desk, you want to have a visual reminder of important dates, responsibilities, and activities; however, you don't have a calendar on which you can write. What alternatives could you use?

• Use a graphic organizer, perhaps a Venn diagram, T-chart, or compare/contrast chart, to compare the use of a hard copy address book and the address book found on computers.

G. Creating and Completing Special Forms

The Internet has many sites to help *adults* with the writing of cover letters and resumés, and these special forms are frequently dealt with at the high school level, too. Seldom, though, are they considered in the elementary grades. Here, I would like to suggest that it is also important for younger students to be introduced to, and given experiences with, the forms that take into account their skills, accomplishments, and educational backgrounds. Students can be taught, as early as Grade 2, how to present these important facts and to complete basic personal data sheets and even simple resumés for age-appropriate jobs, such as raking leaves, walking dogs, and shovelling snow.

I fondly recall a Grade 5 student's response to completing data sheets and filling in skeleton resumés for fictitious jobs. Disconcertedly, the boy wailed, "Boy, I'd better get my butt in gear! My resumé is so awful even *I* wouldn't hire me. Here I am 10 years old and I've done *nothing!* I'm gonna join Scouts and start volunteering at the Seniors' Lodge!" The amazing part was that he *did* do both of those things. Had he not been exposed to personal data collection, it is doubtful he would have.

Another student in the same class was hesitant to list her numerous assets and accomplishments on her data sheet and practice resumé. She was an A student who excelled at many crafts and sports; she was also an excellent babysitter and a Grade 1 tutor. When I asked her why she didn't list these wonderful strengths, her reply was, "That would make me seem stuck up. That would be bad." I explained that she should see what she could do as important successes and that identifying them could have a positive, rather than a negative, influence.

A third student comment served to reinforce my belief that completing private individual data sheets with children is worthwhile. The student studied his completed sheet and then said proudly, "Gee, I didn't know how much I knew. I am pretty smart, after all!" His personal affirmation thrilled me. I knew the resumé he intended to submit to a local gardener in hope of an after-school job cutting lawns would be well received.

These students reaffirmed my conviction that all students need to be taught to think about their own skills, accomplishments, and educational backgrounds, and to learn how to present these data on special forms, including employment applications.

It is never too soon to begin practising these skills and types of thinking. This section of *Real Life Literacy* offers lessons that will allow you to help your students meet these objectives.

22. Personal Data Sheets

VOCABULARY
Data: information, facts, or records
Autobiography: story of self, memoir
Biography: factual story of another person

A personal data sheet is an outline about oneself. It can be used or referred to when seeking a job (even one as elementary as babysitting or raking leaves), writing a resumé, or applying for a scholarship or financial assistance.

Suggested Motivational Set

Play Who Am I? There are two ways to do this.

Make name cards, or index cards with clearly printed names of familiar or easily identified characters. The cards are taped to the front of each child. Allow children several minutes to discuss their new "characters." Children will then answer some questions as their characters, for example: "What is your favorite food?" The Homer Simpson child might answer, "everything"; Wolverine of the X-men might answer, "steaks." Point out how knowing something about characters helps people understand them. Lead the discussion to the idea that students need to know themselves and can create simple personal data sheets.

More challenging alternative: Make index cards as above and attach them to students' backs. Without knowing what names are on their backs, students circulate and ask yes/no questions of their peers in attempts to figure out who they are. Debrief in the same manner as above.

Preparing

1. Ask students to identify five things about themselves that they would like someone whom they have just met and really like to know about them. Have them share the information with peers sitting close by.
2. Lead a discussion about when they might want others to know important information about them. Situations might include
   - meeting new friends, students, or neighbors
   - trying to get a casual job, such as babysitting, dog walking, or yard work
   - meeting a new teacher or leader, such as a coach or group leader
   - presenting oneself for a position in the school, such as class president or school representative
   - applying for a formal job that comes with a consistent salary or rate of pay
3. Brainstorm the various data that would be good to include in such instances. These could include education, interests, previous experience, skills or hobbies, and something about personal characteristics, such as friendly or responsible.

Presenting

4. Use "Personal Data Sheet: Filled-in sample" as an overhead to discuss, teach, or reinforce the idea of creating a personal data sheet. Point out that it is like a "practice run," or like jot notes for completing a job application, a resumé, or even an autobiography.

Practising

5. Provide handouts of the blank data sheet for students to complete.
6. A fun follow-up would be to have students use the information from their data sheets to write brief autobiographies or to exchange data with a peer and write biographies.

Personal Data Sheet: Filled-in sample

Personal Data Sheet

Education: _Graduated from St. Thomas Elementary last year, 2005_
Attending Montgomery Junior High School
Taking music and drama options

Personal Interests, Skills: _acting, public speaking, singing in church choir,_
swimming, ballet (taking lessons)

Clubs or Associations: _Girl Guides for 2 years, Junior choir for 3 years, Junior_
Swimming Club at YWCA for 3 years

Personal Hobbies: _reading, listening to music, writing poetry_

Past Experience: _babysitting (for 2 years for pre-school children), helping_
with Kindergarten Christmas concert, singing for seniors at
McQueen Lodge

Job Interests: _working with children, helping with recitals or dance reviews,_
working at community playgrounds

Personal Data Sheet

Personal Data Sheet

Education: _____

_____

_____

_____

Personal Interests, Skills: _____

_____

_____

_____

Clubs or Associations: _____

_____

_____

_____

Personal Hobbies: _____

_____

_____

_____

Past Experience: _____

_____

_____

_____

Job Interests: _____

_____

_____

_____

23. Resumés

Be sure to teach the previous lesson, Personal Data Sheets, before doing this one.

VOCABULARY
Template: model, pattern, or guide
Resumé: a professional presentation of personal strengths prepared for employment opportunities; in some cases, referred to as a CV (curriculum vitae)
Legible: readable, understandable
Objective: with relation to resumés, the reason for writing and submitting the resume
Relevant: pertinent, having reference to the matter at hand, important
Reference: relating to resumés, this refers to a person who has agreed to provide recommendations for the applicant.

Point out to students that using a template such as the one provided is not the best way to create a resumé and is intended for the learning process only.

Once students reach the age of ten, various paying positions are available to them. That makes the creation of valid resumés more than a preparatory literacy activity; it becomes an authentic pre-employment task and helps instill a valuable work ethic for later years.

Suggested Motivational Set

Play I Am/I Am Not. In pairs, students carry out a conversation by alternately beginning what they say with "I am" or "I am not." After a few minutes, reverse roles so that each student has a chance to begin with both openings. For example:

> *I am a student.*
> *I am not as smart a student as you are.*
> *I am glad to be at school today.*
> *I am not glad to be here because …*

Follow up the game by discussing how students should appreciate both what they are and what they are not. Emphasize that they should select only positive ideas for a resumé.

Preparing

1. Discuss with the class their many responsibilities, including chores, care for siblings, and homework. Ask how many students have been "paid" for a particular activity, and point out that this makes the task a form of employment.
2. Ask if any of the students had to apply for the positions they held. Raise probing questions, for example: "What might happen if two people wanted the same position?" That will lead naturally to a discussion of various ways to present oneself in a positive light.

Presenting

3. Talk about the completion of a personal resumé, and tie it to the previous lesson, Personal Data Sheets.
4. Share the blackline masters "Overview of a Resumé" and "Sample Resumé" on overheads or as individual handouts. Work through the various components together.
5. Discuss the concept of references. It is better not to include references with a resume, but students should be prepared to provide letters on request. Students might include reference names and phone numbers, just names, or a line like "References available on request" depending on the level of concern about privacy and security.
6. Discuss cover letters. Point out that they are necessary with official job applications and that in all instances are viewed as a persuasive tool.
7. Brainstorm important points to remember when completing a personal resumé. For example:
   - Write or print legibly. If using a computer, use a clear, easy-to-read font.
   - Be completely honest. If you do not have accurate information and are making an "educated" guess, indicate this.

- Maintain the professional appearance of the document by doing your best not to fold or crumple it.
- If you use other people as references, be sure to get their permission.
- If possible, make each reference specific to the position for which you are applying.
- Identify your objective in submitting the resumé.
- Be concise and to the point. Many places prefer one-page resumés.
- Emphasize personal positive characteristics that will be needed for the specific position.
- Identify memberships in clubs, groups, or extracurricular activities because these show you to be a well-rounded person; however, avoid listing interests that may be questionable (e.g., "like watching a lot of TV").
- Include any volunteering you have done, both that which may be mandatory for high school graduation and that which is self-motivated.
- Edit carefully—spelling and grammar must be perfect.

Practising

8. Allow younger students to fill in the "Resumé Template" blackline master. Older students can create a resumé without the template. Suggest that they complete the resumé for a position of interest to them (e.g., babysitting, assisting in a home, delivering flyers).

9. A fun follow-up is to have students create a resumé for an imaginary position using imaginary qualifications. For example, a student could pretend to be the world's greatest stunt person, applying to work for Steven Spielberg on his latest adventure movie.

Overview of a Resumé

Contact Information:

• List name, address, phone/fax number, and e-mail address.

Objective:

• Briefly indicate the reason for submitting the resumé.

Education:

• Begin with your most recent education and work backwards. Include both names and addresses of educational institutions.

• Including your "marks" is optional, but depending on the type of position, some employers might conclude that your average is low if you do not disclose them.

• If you have taken any course relevant to the position you are applying for, mention it.

Relevant Experience:

• List any experience beginning with the most recent and working backwards. Include the name of the person you worked for, your "title" (e.g., "dog walker") and your responsibilities.

• Include volunteer activities here, if they apply.

Interests, Skills:

• List hobbies, activities, or clubs with which you are or have been involved—doing so lets a prospective employer know more about you.

• Be concise. Avoid using sentences. Use point form.

References:

• Provide names and contact information for two to four persons who have agreed to serve as references for you; alternatively, insert the line "References available upon request."

Sample Resumé

Kenny Jordan (age 10)
12345–99 St. Newton, MB R4E 7Y8
455 304-5732
kdjordan@shaw.ca

I would like an outdoor, yard work position:
- raking leaves
- cutting grass
- shovelling snow

Education:

Hillard Elementary School, St. Grove Ave., Newton, MB
Grades 2–5: now in Grade 5
Passed Grade 4 with an 86% average

Brittania Elementary, N 120 St., Newton, MB
Grade 1

McQueen Kindergarten, 10909-45 Ave., Newton, MB
Kindergarten

Relevant Experience:
- Worked last fall for Mr. Anderson, raking his leaves
- Helped my grandfather shovel walks last winter
- Have helped my dad rake leaves every fall
- Earned Scouts Canada badges in outdoor awareness and orienteering

Interests, Skills:
- Like being outside, camping, hiking, riding my bike
- Play hockey and baseball (Little League) yearly
- Belong to Scouts Canada
- Belong to the Junior Marshall Arts Club

References:
- John Dawson, neighbor, 14345 99 St., Newton, MB M2R 3T6
  455 304-7689
- Larry Anderson, family friend, 99 Tower Cres., Newton, MB M8Y 1T8
  607 234-6654
- Rev. K. Marshall, St. Mary's Church, 44 St. N 123 Ave., Newton, MB M9T 2R7
  604 110-9867

Resumé Template

For drafting only

Name _____

Address _____

Phone & fax _____

E-mail _____

Objective: _____

Education: _____

_____

_____

_____

Relevant Experience: _____

_____

_____

_____

Interests, Skills: _____

_____

_____

_____

References: _____

_____

_____

_____

24. Employment Applications

VOCABULARY
Applicant: a hopeful, a contender
Employment: service, work

Since at some points in their lives all students will be faced with the task of getting a job, teaching them how to complete generic employment applications and giving them practice in doing so is an authentic literacy activity. Although every application differs according to the employer's needs, there are enough generalities to make the activity valid.

Suggested Motivational Set

Invite students to write or print a message in the messiest script possible. Have them exchange their notes with peers and try to decipher one another's messages. Now, talk about people with messy writing—notoriously, doctors or perhaps one of their parents—and possible problems that might result. Discuss when perfect printing is important, and lead into the topic of completing an employment application. Draw to their attention the fact that on most applications, printing is requested and is likely to be neater than cursive writing.

Preparing

1. Invite students to share information about any small jobs they have done. These can be as tiny as assisting the teacher hand out materials or helping with home chores.
2. Brainstorm the possible jobs students might have (e.g., babysitting, dog walking, yard work, peer tutoring).
3. Ask how students get those jobs and then ask the students how they think adults get jobs. "Is it the same way?" Attempt to draw from the students the idea of applying for a job, but be prepared to offer it, if necessary.
4. Discuss all the areas where students might have to fill in applications in order to belong to something or take part in specific activities. These areas include volunteering and joining specialized clubs or teams, in addition to the more usual positions of paid employment.

Presenting

5. Share the next blackline master as an overhead, going over the various areas in need of completion. Choose whichever is most appropriate for your students.
6. Brainstorm the important points to remember—these are similar to "resumés"—and list if necessary.

Practising

See Lesson 25, Cover Letters, for more on writing convincing and effective cover letters.

7. For individual practice, provide students with blank copies of these blackline masters: "Generic Application for Employment," "Resumé Template," and "Personal Data Sheet." For "fun" allow them to create fantasy jobs and equally fantastical personal characteristics that will make them the best possible selections for the positions.

Generic Application for Employment

Application for Employment

[The name and address of the company or person doing the employing will be here.]

Please complete the entire application.

1. Personal Information (please print)

Name   Social Insurance/Security Number   Date (M/D/Y)

Last   First

Other names you are known by _____   Are you less than 18? Yes ___ No ___

Present Address

Street   City   Province/State   Postal Code/Zip Code

Present Address

Street   City   Province/State   Postal Code/Zip Code

Phone Number _____ _____   Referred by _____
         Daytime   Evening

2. Employment Desired

Position   Location/Department   Salary Desired   Date Available

Specify hours available each week.
Sun. ____ Mon. ____ Tues. ____ Wed. ____ Thurs. ____ Fri. ____ Sat. ____

Are you able to work overtime? _____

Have you ever worked with this company before? ____ If yes, when? _____

3. Education

	Name/Address of School	Last Year Completed	Graduate Y? N?
High School			
Post Secondary			
Specific Related Courses			

List skills relevant to position applied for. _____

4. Objectives

Please describe briefly why you are seeking employment here.

_____

_____

_____

25. Cover Letters

Applicant: person seeking a job or position

Employer: the person or group of persons who are hiring others to work for them

Employee: the person working for someone else

Qualifications: related experience, education, or training

Recipient: person or persons to whom the letter is addressed

Submission: whatever is being sent to, or given to, another person for examination

Generic: general, standard, or nonspecific

Recommendation: approval or praise

Although Language Arts curricula include numerous lessons on letter writing, the writing of cover letters is probably less considered. Teaching students how to write the best possible cover letters for specific situations would be constructive and strengthen real-life literacy. Even the youngest students can begin putting their ideas in cover letter format.

Suggested Motivational Set

Share the following scenario with the students.

> *Your parents are going to hire an older student as a tutor to help you with some difficulties in mathematics. They want you to decide who your tutor should be based on two cover letters that students have sent in reply to their advertisement. Only the bodies of the letters are shown here. For this situation, your name is David. Which person would you choose? Why?*

Share both "Cover Letter A" and "Cover Letter B" orally, or make them into overheads for viewing. (See pages 114 and 115.) Discuss as a class the reasons for choosing one letter over another. Lead the discussion towards the idea of "positive presentation" of self, pointing out how the writer of Letter B seems more enthusiastic, even though this person may not be as qualified. Since there is no right or wrong choice, allow lots of open discussion about both letters.

Preparing

1. Discuss the concept of cover letters, being sure to reinforce the purpose of such letters. Emphasize that a cover letter is the chance for the writer to highlight important qualifications, to catch the attention of the reader, and to draw attention to personal strengths that will directly affect the position being sought. Most cover letters accompany resumés for job applications, but these letters serve other purposes as well. For instance, a cover letter might accompany an article for submission to a newspaper or magazine, or a letter of recommendation or appreciation.

2. Brainstorm different jobs in which the students may be interested and that might require cover letters. (Younger students may consider writing cover letters to parents to accompany report cards.)

3. Discuss vocabulary if desired.

Presenting

4. As a class, brainstorm what might be included in a good cover letter. Ensure that the following ideas are brought forward.
   - Make every attempt to address the letter to a real person, as opposed to falling back on "To whom it may concern." If you are unable to locate a name, try to find out the position, for example, superintendent or director, and use that. The letter is less likely to be overlooked if directed to a specific person.
   - Make sure your letter directly addresses the needs of the employer or concerns of the recipient. Avoid writing a basic, standard letter that could be sent to anyone. Include explicit references to the particular situation or position.

- Be sure to include examples of your own success that relate specifically to the position or situation. Here is a chance to "look great."
- Keep the letter positive and enthusiastic. Remember that the recipient will get excited about you and your letter only if the letter is written with passion. Use positive words that will demonstrate your eagerness. For example, rather than writing "I think I might be good at …," say "I know I will be successful at …" Express yourself in the way that seems most engaging.
- Outline exactly why you are writing and what you want to accomplish. For example, if you are applying for a position, say that; if you are writing to make a recommendation, say that. Be sure that the recipient will easily be able to determine your reason for writing.
- Trust your own voice in the cover letter. In other words, avoid being overly formal—write in a way that shows who you are. Remember that the letter should be neither "chatty" nor solemn. It should be interesting to read.
- If seeking a job, ask for an interview; if making a query letter, request a reply.
- Be sure grammar, spelling, and punctuation are perfect. Similarly, be sure that any information provided is accurate and not misleading in any way.

5. Review the rules of letter writing, as appropriate for your grade level. Point out that a cover letter is a form of business letter, so should be relatively formal and precise. Remind students that to be effective, a cover letter needs to reflect their own voices.

6. Since the concept of cover letter is probably new to students, have the whole class work together to write a model cover letter.

Practising

7. Have students write cover letters of their own, possibly for one of the following scenarios.
- You are submitting a poem, short story, or essay, preferably something recently written in class, to a local newspaper for probable publication.
- You are applying for a part-time position you saw advertised on a poster in the local supermarket. Choose a position in which you are interested.
- You are taking home your first report card of the term, and your marks are not as good as your parents expected.
- You are sending a product critique to the manufacturers. The critique is for a type of sneakers that you and your friends have discovered "fall apart" quickly. You have put together a two-page critique, but need a cover letter to go with it.
- You are applying for a part-time position at a fast-food restaurant.

Cover Letter A

I am replying to your advertisement for a mathematics tutor. You will see from my resume that I am currently employed part time at my father's law office, but my hours there are flexible.

I am in the Honors Program at Western High School; my current core subject average is 94%. Mathematics is my favorite subject so I feel very qualified to assist David with his mathematics difficulties. I am also extremely computer literate and might be able to share mathematics programs that would be of interest to David. I think I can be of great help to him with his math.

I am available any night after 6 p.m. with the exception of Sundays. I am able to begin as early as next week. I look forward to hearing from you soon.

Cover Letter B

I am applying for the position of David's math tutor. I am in Mc Kensy High in Grade 11. You will see from my resume that I don't have a job at the moment, but that I volunteer at the Boys and Girls' Club on Wednesday evenings.

I have a younger brother who also needs a lot of help with his math, so I feel well able to help David. In addition, I have struggled with math myself in the past, so I know how frustrating that can be.

I really like kids. It is my hope to be a camp counselor this summer, and eventually to work with young people in some capacity in the future. At present I am earning my general High School diploma with the intention of going to college to pursue a career in youth counseling.

I am eager to start helping David. I'm sure we can be successful together and in no time David will be enjoying more success in math. Thank you for considering my application; I can hardly wait to hear from you.

Questions for Discussion and Review

• Create and implement a questionnaire that will provide you with information about what specific possible employers are looking for in employees. For example, ask your parents what they would want in a "garage cleaner" or a "garden weeder." Based on what you discover, create an employment application form.

• Explain how you would indicate your education on an employment application.

• You would like to deliver the local monthly newspaper and are filling in an application form. It asks for "related experience." Which of the following would you include on the form, and why?

    Worked at a Supermarket in the summer, tidying shelves

    Have been babysitting for 4 years

    Delivered school flyers to the community

    Sold Girl Guide cookies door-to-door

    Helped my dad with autumn garden clean-up

    Belong to the school Track and Field Club

    Ride a bike in my spare time

    Sing in the school choir

    Went with my mom when she was going door-to-door doing the census last year

    Delivered groceries every week to the seniors in McQueen Lodge last summer

• You want to use your last year's teacher as a reference on an application for a position in a local choir. How will you do this?

• Explain the "objective" of a personal resumé. How long should this be? Write a possible objective for a position of volunteering at a seniors' home.

• What is the purpose of a personal data sheet? What should be included on it?

• List five important points to remember when writing a resumé or filling in a job application.

• Explain how a cover letter is both the same as, and different from, a regular business letter. Write a sentence for a cover letter that shows a positive attitude and enthusiasm for the positions of cook at a fast-food restaurant, babysitter, dog walker, and car washer at a local car wash.

H. Approaches to Authentic, Everyday Teaching

In every classroom, teachers may struggle to keep activities relevant, authentic, and motivating to students. Although I realize that not all tasks can be highly inspiring, this section offers suggestions for keeping many of these as meaningful and as close to real-life literacy as possible. In addition, I have included thoughts on "being an authentic professional and colleague." Although these ideas are not directly related to literacy, they are important when considering the relevant and influential stance of your role as a teacher.

Unlike the preceding six sections of the book, this final section does not follow the "prepare, present, practise" approach; instead, it lists ways in which you can effectively address issues related to authentic teaching. By *authentic teaching*, I mean teaching that ties learning and practice to real-life experiences. Whereas the real-life literacy lessons in the preceding pages automatically fit these guidelines, other in-class activities may not. I offer suggestions that I hope will help with these situations.

Creating Authentic Resources

In attempts to save money and have exactly what they want for specific lessons, teachers frequently end up making many of the resources used in classrooms. Unfortunately, long hours spent in preparation of materials does not necessarily mean the results will be as positive as expected. Perhaps, the problem is that the teacher-made supplies are not as authentic as they could be. I hope the following suggestions will give you some ideas for teacher-made resources that are well worth the time required to assemble.

- Photo Stories: These mini-books or worksheets are made with photographs of the staff or students and can be used over and over again for a variety of literacy-based purposes. (Be sure to get consent to copy from the "models.")
- Class Narrative: A single story written to include each class member in some manner, can, like the photo story, be used in many authentic ways. If you are not creative, choose a popular story or poem and strategically add students' names. Tales with many characters, perhaps Snow White and the *Twenty-seven* Dwarfs, work the best; however, any story can be adapted to include more "groups" of characters. This is highly motivating and authentic for children.
- Music Selections: The creation of audiotapes or CDs of carefully selected tunes, with and without words, can be used indefinitely. If a tape or CD is put together with care and thought, a single collection can be used for many purposes:

- promoting relaxation
- as a background to silent work
- keeping rhythm
- energizing students
- singing along to
- writing or thinking about (lyrics)
- scene setting (e.g., sounds of storms for stories)
- doing creative movement

• Creative Clozes: A collection of familiar quotes, sayings, or sentences, kept together in one file folder, can be a great source of sentences for cloze activities, where students examine missing words or phrases to predict, create, or spell.

• Calendar Overheads: With so many wonderful calendars from which to choose, the biggest problem will be making the best selection. Once you choose your favorite calendar, make colored overheads of each of the pictures, or mount and laminate the pictures, and file away for future use to promote discussion, thinking, writing, illustrating, and more.

• Student Work Anthologies: By collecting samples of students' work, obtaining permission for their use, and binding them into a book format, you will have a valuable, authentic resource for in-class use in the silent reading area or for a "read-to" listening situation.

Creating Authentic In-Class Writing Tasks

Teachers know how important it is for all students to write daily, but sometimes it is difficult to come up with real reasons for doing so. Although I am the first to admit there are many instances when writing practice is simply that—practice—real-life writing assignments will promote the development of good writing skills. The following are a few examples of such writing.

• To Do Lists: Students create lists of what they actually have to do. These might include school-related tasks, home chores, people to contact for some particular reason such as invitations or thank-you notes, and preparations for a particular event. Notes could even be more global and feature life or future-related goals.

• Writing Steps: Have students write prioritized steps to completing something important to them, such as getting better marks, washing a dog, learning a sport, or making a meal.

• I-Am-Innocent: Have students think of a time when they were "assumed guilty," but were really innocent. Perhaps something was broken, missing, or moved from where it should be. Invite them to write, in point or paragraph form, the reasons why they believe they were unfairly judged. (Often in life, we have to prove our innocence, so this activity is very true to life.)

• Memory Helper: Invite students to brainstorm times, events, places, or people that they want to remember; they then create an appropriate list, calendar, or organizer of their design to facilitate this.

• Logging My Moods: Invite students to keep a journal record of their feelings—what makes them happy, angry, sad, and more—over a set period of time. Professionals often suggest this activity to improve self-understanding, so it serves as a useful, real-life writing activity for students, as well.

• What I Want to Say: Have students write exactly what they want to say to a specific person, either on the phone or in person, before they say it. This real-life preparatory activity prevents common mistakes in conversation. The writing could be "what I want to say to" a friend, peer, teacher, parent, relative, other adult or even to a stranger if, for example, the student was selling something or canvassing door to door.

• Gentle Persuasion: Discuss instances when gentle persuasion helps put one's point across. Examples might include encouraging parents to allow a later bedtime or an increase in allowance. Invite students to make a written copy of how they will present their cases.

• Putting It Back Together: Often, we take something apart and then forget how to put it back together—fixing a bike tire is an example. Discuss when this has happened or might happen in the future. (Most students will have at least witnessed this frustrating activity at home.) Encourage them to write the steps to taking something apart, then to reverse these and write them in such a way to facilitate putting the item back together. These situations could include

  • bikes (tires, chains)
  • CD players or VCRs
  • school binders (notes, pages, dividers)
  • specific toys

Making Worksheets Meaningful

Teachers have long been cautioned about the pitfalls of worksheets, yet most of us realize that they are a necessity for specific situations. By incorporating any or several of these ideas on your "teacher-made" worksheets, at least some of the downsides will be avoided.

• Use students' real names.

• Write the sheets about authentic situations: for example, if reviewing punctuation, write about a recent classroom activity.

• Use a story format: write each individual sentence as a separate part of an ongoing story, or even copy sentences from a familiar story for use on, for example, a grammar worksheet.

• Tell jokes or share funny class anecdotes on the worksheet, either as part of the work or as hidden addons scattered around the page.

• Write the worksheet as clues to a mystery. For example, answers could be united to form a "clue." The mystery could be based on situations such as where is a missing item, what did someone do last night, or who wrote the message on the board.

• Use cloze technique *within* the questions you pose. For example, when asking about the protagonist's motivation, write "Why did Pe_ _ _ steal the d_g?"

• Write the questions or sentences such that some responses are silly, obvious, or nonsensical. For example, on a worksheet practising capitalization, you might write, "Our principal, mr knowles, lives on bard street with his 77 wives."

Encouraging Authentic Cooperative Challenges

It has been proven that in-class cooperative learning promotes positive interdependence, individual accountability, and spontaneous interaction, as well as social and group processing skills. However, it has also been demonstrated that some degree of "competition" is positive and stimulating to most students. In *cooperative challenges*, the cooperative spirit within groups works in the context of a small element of low-risk competition between groups, as in each case the groups "challenge" each other to "create a better…." If desired, at commencement of separate tasks, each group chooses a "tribunal member" to sit on a panel to determine the best project or outcome. Tribunal members can't vote for their own groups, but can take part in all discussions and attempt to sway other voters through dialogue. The activities are authentic in that each involves either the students or something specific or important to them. For example, students deal with familiar concerns or dilemmas in fun, motivating ways and usually reach some form of solution—this is real-life problem solving.

• Theatre Sports: Revival of this well-used activity for classroom use capitalizes on the merits of cooperation as group members improvise situations suggested by the tribunal council. (One scenario is three people and one bus seat.)

• A Story of Us: Each group composes, writes, and then shares a short story in which members are the protagonists.

• Our School: Groups try to create the most captivating and informative posters representing their school.

• Perfect Teacher: Groups discuss, brainstorm, and draw or write about the qualities of a perfect (imaginary) teacher. (Teachers will find this a good learning experience!) *Note:* "Perfect Friend" or "Perfect Parent" can be substituted.

• An Action Plan: Based on a specific school need, dilemma, or concern, groups write action plans for dealing with the situation. Topics might range from the need for more volleyballs to the need to reduce bullying. The plans can later be shared with the principal if desired.

• Directions for Dummies: As in the popular "… for Dummies" series, groups create a simplified, easy-to-follow set of directions for either first graders or new-to-the-school students, to facilitate their familiarity with the school and its many idiosyncrasies, such as "where the Grade 6'ers meet."

• Future Seers: Groups design posters, stories, or fact charts that are representative of schools of the future.

• Support Groups: Groups determine where in the school or local community they can "lend a hand," write up a plan, put it into action, and then write a reflection. Some lend-a-hand ideas might be cleaning up part of the playground, helping a Kindergarten teacher, assisting the custodian with garbage emptying, collecting the school recycling for a week, delivering teachers' mail to their rooms, or serving as study buddies with younger students.

Being a Teaching Colleague in Authentic Ways

There is more to working in a school setting than just being a classroom teacher; it is necessary to be a colleague as well, and being an important and authentic supporter of peers is not always easy. Some teachers appear to be naturals. They blend beautifully into any school environment and almost immediately become integral cogs in the wheel of that school. Others, perhaps due to personality, confidence levels, or learning styles, have more difficulty working authentically with peers. This is to be expected. It would be boring if we were all the same. However, there are some conscious changes or activities any teacher can carry out to improve his or her authenticity as a colleague.

• Keep a personal record of colleagues' special dates. These include birthdays, religious celebrations, and anniversaries.

- Practise being a bright light rather than a dusty bulb in the staff room. It's just as easy to smile as to frown, and everyone benefits.
- Avoid being a loner. When you actively seek the help of your peers, you put value on their skills and judgment. (On the other hand, avoid becoming over-dependent on any staff member.)
- Offer assistance, but only if you are truly prepared to give it. Be true to your words and promises.
- Attend staff get-togethers, at least occasionally, even if this is "not your thing." To avoid doing so suggests that you feel you are not part of a team.
- Consider yourself part of a team, as opposed to part of a competition. Avoid getting into a situation of one-upmanship with a colleague.
- Remind yourself not to take the view that it is "staff against students." The entire school body will function more efficiently if there are no "sides."
- Be on the alert for signs of stress in peers, and, if appropriate, offer assistance or support. Be prepared to follow through.
- Occasionally, surprise a colleague with a treat, such as a flower, a special cup of coffee, or a pile of copying done. Include support staff in your definition of colleague. Remember that true compassion is not based on receiving appreciation for what has been done. Keep the treat anonymous.
- Recognize and acknowledge the importance of support staff. Remember "Administrative Professionals Day," even if only with a few kind words of appreciation. Make positive comments to the custodian about his or her care for the school.

Acting as an Authentic School Advocate

We are professionals. Our schools are our places of work and whether or not we are *overjoyed* with the physical make-up or internal workings of these institutions, it is our professional obligation to stand behind them and support them. I will never forget overhearing a novice teacher "running down the way her *old, decrepit* school was *principaled.*" The teacher spoke in a public area and many others, some of whom happened to be community parents, listened in. It was a travesty, not only for the teacher, but for the school, the children who attended it, and their parents. As teachers, we must always serve as sincere advocates for our schools. The following are suggestions on how to ensure this.

- Create a list—a good whole-class brainstorming activity—of the "positives" about your school. These may include physical attributes, such as a great playground; curriculum-based features, perhaps an excellent Mathematics program; extracurricular attributes, such as a good soccer team; and staff, for example, the presence of a friendly secretary. Doing this ensures that you will always have ready a few positives to share about the school wherever you are.
- Have your students create posters, bulletins, flyers, or brochures that promote the school and applaud its positive features.
- Write a brief bulletin commending your school. Publish it in a school bulletin or newspaper or send it to a local newspaper. Often, newspapers are quite willing to publish such positive articles. Or, if your students are old enough, invite them to do this, make a "composite" of their positive comments, and send it for publication.
- Attend extracurricular functions as much as possible. For example, cheer your school at a game, even if it is after hours, or support them at a drama production,

even if you had no part in its preparation. A positive appearance, even occasionally, goes a long way towards promoting school advocacy.

• Accept and promote the school philosophy. As long as you are employed there, it is the philosophy under which you work.

• Attend school meetings with a positive attitude. No one enjoys meetings, but being there with a negative or surly outlook is bad for everyone. Remember that it is easier to smile than to frown.

• Show respect for the principal, especially in public, even if you don't always agree with that person. Speak only of his or her positive attributes. Be especially conscious of this during parent–teacher interviews.

• Wear school clothing or logos proudly.

• Treat the building(s) and grounds of your school with as much care as you would your own home. Make it a point to encourage students to do the same.

• Talk often with students about the strengths of your school. Accept the limitations, but avoid dwelling on them.

• Promote and diligently follow school rules. Not to do so demonstrates disrespect for the school and its leaders.

• Avoid getting caught up in any negative shop talk about your school, even if you inwardly agreed with what was said. Remember that words spoken cannot be reclaimed. It is better to remain quiet and speak positively when possible.

Appendix A: Postal Abbreviations

This teacher resource material supports Lesson 10, Package Labels, Addresses, and Special Post Forms. It relates to Steps 5 and Step 7 under Presenting.

Canadian Provinces and Territories: Shortforms

British Columbia: BC
Alberta: AB
Saskatchewan: SK
Manitoba: MB
Ontario: ON
Quebec: QU
Newfoundland & Labrador: NL
Prince Edward Island: PE
Nova Scotia: NS
Nunavut: NU
Yukon: YT
Northwest Territories: NT

U.S. States and Possessions: Shortforms

Alabama: AL
Alaska: AK
American Samoa: AS
Arizona: AZ
Arkansas: AR
California: CA
Colorado: CO
Connecticut: CT
Delaware: DE
District of Columbia: DC
Federated States of Micronesia: FM
Florida: FL
Georgia: GA
Guam: GU
Hawaii: HI
Idaho: ID
Illinois: IL
Indiana: IN
Iowa: IA
Kansas: KS
Kentucky: KY
Louisiana: LA
Maine: ME
Marshall Islands: MH
Maryland: MD

Massachusetts: MA
Michigan: MI
Minnesota: MN
Mississippi: MS
Missouri: MO
Montana: MT
Nebraska: NE
Nevada: NV
New Hampshire: NH
New Jersey: NJ
New Mexico: NM
New York: NY
North Carolina: NC
North Dakota: ND
Northern Mariana Islands: MP
Ohio: OH
Oklahoma: OK
Oregon: OR
Palau: PW
Pennsylvania: PA
Puerto Rico: PR
Rhode Island: RI
South Carolina: SC
South Dakota: SD
Tennessee: TN
Texas: TX
Utah: UT
Vermont: VT
Virginia: VA
Washington: WA
West Virginia: WV
Wisconsin: WI
Wyoming: WY

Major Street Types

Note: (E) signifies English; (F) signifies French.
Avenue: AVE (E) AV (F)
Boulevard: BLVD (E) BOUL (F)
Centre: CTR (E) C (F)
Court: CRT
Crescent: CRES
Freeway: FWY

Heights: HTS
Mountain: MTN
Park: PK
Parkway: PKY
Place: PL (E) PLACE (F)
Point: PT
Private: PVT
Road: RD
Square: SQ
Subdivision: SUBDIV

Unit Designators

Apartment: APT
Suite: SUITE
Unit: UNIT

Directional Abbreviations

East: E
North: N
Northeast: NE

South: S
Southeast: SE
Southwest: SW
West: W

Delivery Installation Types

Post Office: PO
Retail Postal Outlet: RPO
Station: STN
Letter Carrier Depot: LCD
Community Mail Centre: CMC
Commercial Dealership Outlet: CDO

Mode of Delivery Designation

General Delivery: GD
Mobile Route: MR
Post Office Box: PO BOX
Rural Route: RR
Suburban Service: SS

Appendix B: The Hidden Ingredients in Product Labels

This teacher resource material relates to Lesson 7, Food Product Labels.

Sometimes, food labels use words that disguise or obscure true product content. You may wish to alert your students to the presence of certain ingredients in common foods. For health reasons, ingredients, such as salt, are best eaten in limited quantities. Be sure to remind students that all ingredients are okay in moderation. They may even be necessary or beneficial in small amounts. The problem is their presence is not always obvious.

Students should learn vocabulary that indicates the presence of certain ingredients and consider the amount of the ingredient as listed on a food label. The provided lists identify common foods that are likely to contain salt, trans fats, sugar, refined or enriched grains, and empty calories in what I have referred to as "possibly problematic" quantities.

Salt

The presence of salt is indicated by the words "sodium," "monosodium glutamate," "baking soda," and "baking powder." Salt is often found in "possibly problematic" quantities in
- canned soups
- frozen meals
- some cereals
- pizza
- fast foods
- bread
- baked goods (e.g., pastries, donuts)
- canned vegetables
- pickles and olives
- some pre-packaged snack foods (e.g., potato chips, pretzels)
- deli cold cuts
- soy sauce

Trans Fat

The presence of trans fat is indicated by such words as "hydrogenated oil," "saturated fat," "unsaturated fatty acids," "partially hydrogenated," and "shortening." It is often found in "possibly problematic" quantities in
- fried foods (e.g., French fries)
- hard butter or margarine
- cookies, cakes, and crackers
- cheese
- snack foods (e.g., potato chips, microwave popcorn)

Sugar

The presence of sugar is disguised by its many forms, including dextrose, fructose, sucrose, corn syrup, sorghum, maltose, glucose, honey, molasses, and evaporated cane or fruit juice. It is often found in "possibly problematic" quantities in

- soda pop
- sweetened cereal
- "light" peanut butter (has more sugar than regular peanut butter)
- baked goods and sweet desserts
- condiments (e.g., ketchup)
- canned fruits
- jams
- health food bars, protein bars

Refined or Enriched Grains

These appear in enriched flour, unbleached white flour, wheat flour, and de-germed cornmeal. They are often found in "possibly problematic" quantities in

- tortillas
- noodles
- white bread and some "brown" breads (check the labels)
- cornbread
- crackers
- pasta, macaroni
- some dry cereals
- white rice
- bagels
- cereal bars

Empty Calories

These are often disguised as energy, carbohydrates, and fats. They can be found in "possibly problematic" quantities in

- cupcakes, cakes, and cookies
- cinnamon rolls, muffins, and donuts
- gravies, some sauces
- salad dressings, mayonnaise, mustard, ketchup
- some snack foods
- soda pop
- energy drinks or bars

Index